I0551588

Greetings Notes Readers!
Welcome to this wonderful summer issue!
Folks must have family and relationships on the mind. As we editors began poring over the short stories and personal essays we liked for this issue, we found that most were linked by an unintended theme!

We didn't set out to put together a 'theme' issue but we like to go with the flow at Notes! So we present you with issue #5- full of surprises and happy accidents! It must've been fate....With heat waves and sunstroke, tempers running as high as other appetites, and unquenchable needs for refreshments-- we've got something for all your summertime blues...

Even our cover is a family affair!

Our Editor-in-Chief also happens to be a photoshop buff. A few weeks back she found 2 separate doodles hanging around the house. The 1st was a sensational cat woman, drawn by Harmoni's 13 year old daughter, Blayse Howard. So Harmoni got to thinking, was planning to play some with it—*then* she found a 2nd doodle. This was an interesting sort of collage drawn by her own mother, Sheryl Keith. Now the inspiration was really flowing! These separate elements were combined and tinkered with, in whole-hearted enjoyment, and *voila!* issue #5's cover art was born!

Here's to happy accidents, hot days, warm nights, and spending them with the folks you love!

The Editors
Notes Magazine
Grace Notes Publishing

Author Du Jour

House Specialties

A La Carte

White Fields and Emerson

by Saul Lemerond

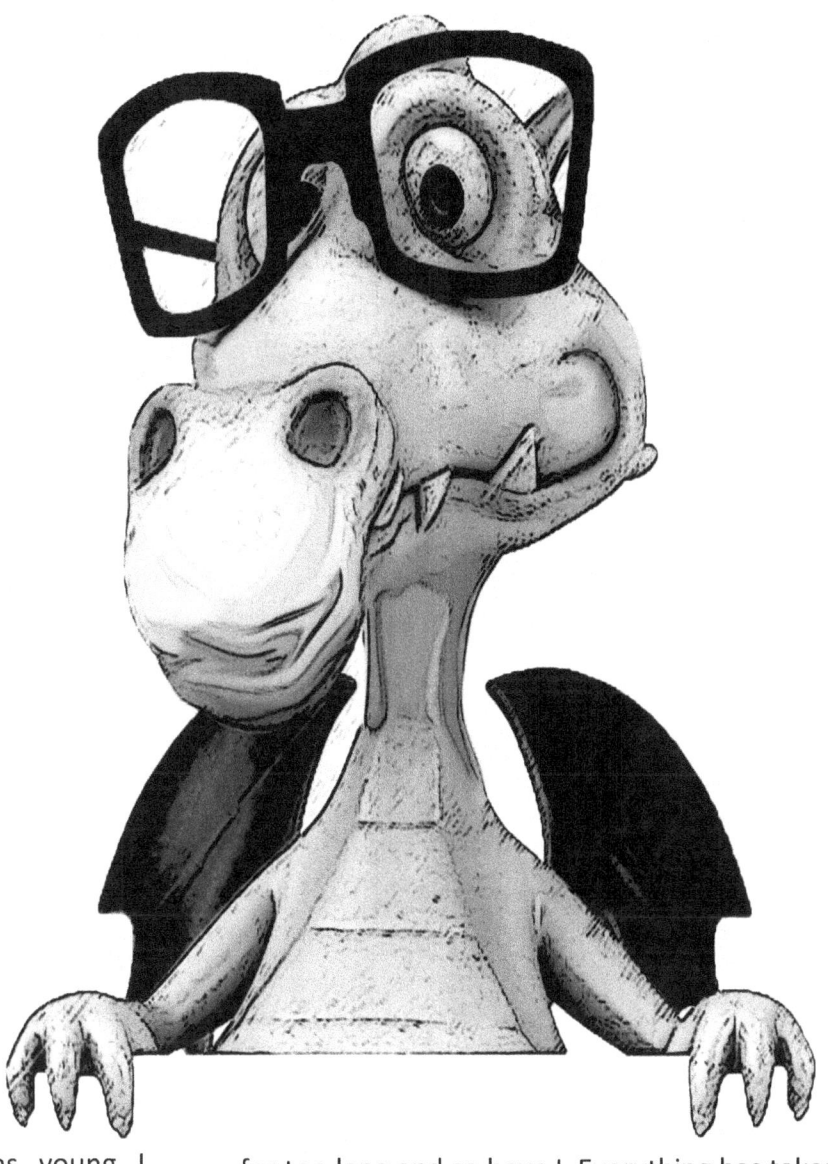

It seems to me all the smart life took a cue from evolution and beat feet south or decided to take a four-month nap. Not us humans, though. Our brains have made us stupid and the cold makes us more so. Every winter I feel a primal urge to migrate south and when I fail to do this, my body does its best to hibernate and wishes it was a dinosaur.

A dinosaur of transcendence.

So I'm in a frozen field of gray and white, trying to transcend. Emerson says, "It is the quality of the moment, not the number of days, or events, or of actors, that imports." I take this to mean that I should try to be happy even though I believe that the only animal capable of happiness during a Wisconsin winter is the penguin, and we don't have penguins in Wisconsin, and I'm not a penguin. Although, when I was young I wanted to be a dinosaur. I'm sorry, that's a lie. I still want to be a dinosaur. Even with the small arms and hands of a Tyrannosaurus rex, winter would be far more tolerable. Sure, there would be some difficulty in throwing snowballs, but really, who is going to start a snowball fight with a T-rex? Even if someone did, it would make this colorless field more interesting when I ate them.

The snow is as white as white and the wind is cold. It's February, the northern quarter of the United States has been without enough sun for too long and so have I. Everything has taken on its own particular shade of gray. This is partially because snow has covered the brown grass and evergreens and partially because the salt has drifted from the roads to cover everything else.

Perhaps some sort of image would help, like maybe something red. It might make this field somewhat more manageable. Red and white go together, don't they? I forget what red looks like. The dinosaurs never had this problem, and I'm jealous because the earth was warm yet when they walked around in their tropical Pangaea.

There is an intense reflection from the Sun off of the snow, but this, of course, does not add any color. The Sun's too far away from the earth and its light is different. It's a gray quality, a compact florescent light bulb quality, bright and ugly and not quite the right quality. Not the most ideal of combinations because one always accentuates the others (the bright makes the ugly uglier and the ugly makes the gray grayer, and this all goes a long way to making everything look as though it would look better if it looked some other way) which causes an ever worsening cycle of the three elements getting stronger and then feeding back into each other until all observers have soaked in so much gray that they can't even recognize it anymore. It's inside them now. Internalized. They think that this is the way it has always been. This is the way the earth looks. This is all the natural color I have ever known. I have no reason to expect otherwise. Brilliance is a fantasy and the dinosaurs are dead.

A car, a dusty back car, drives past on the street behind me and a rusty tracker behind it.

The air is dry and cold and smells like restaurant grease and car exhaust and the only sound comes from wind and passing cars thumping their bass. There is no life and no color, nope, only people gorging themselves on Burger King as they move from place to place on gray roads in cars shaded the same, and I try to imagine non-gray.

My bones feel tired. Apparently the body feels it must conserve energy for times when I can wake up to the sound of playing squirrels and singing birds and smell fresh cut grass as I watch bumblebees gather pollen from blooming flowers that I distinctly remember as having color.

I make an effort to count the number of things I can see that are gray. I stop when I get to the number one and decide to try and imagine what the same field looks like in the summer. I conjure a beach ball in the center of the empty field resting gently atop the snow. Probably the beach ball is an improvement, so I leave it there and wonder if what I've done is transcendental.

Maybe, I think. I think maybe I've put a beach ball in this field because I wished to live deliberately, to front only the essential facts of life, and see if I could not learn what it had to teach, and not, when I came to die, discover that I had not lived.

Having worked this out, I move the beach ball two feet to the left of its previous spot and change it from a beach ball to a dinosaur. Specifically, a Tyrannosaurus Rex. I name him Rex. A transcendental name.

Rex turns his scaly head to me and begins to speak.

"A single footstep will not make a path on the earth, so a single thought will not make a pathway in the mind. To make a deep physical path, we walk again and again. To make a deep mental path, we must think over and over the kind of thoughts we wish to dominate our lives."

Rex is right.

I give him a nice big recliner, bifocals, a smoking jacket, a fireplace, a bookcase, and a beach ball.

"You're a T-rex," I point out. "A single one of your footsteps would make a path for me." He puts on his jacket. "Your argument then," I continue, "is inconsistent."

Rex sits down in his chair next to the fireplace, takes a book off the shelf, and affixes his bifocals.

"A foolish consistency," he says once he has found the correct page, "is the hobgoblin of Tyrannosaurus Rex."

He stands for a moment, then lumbers over to the wood bin where he picks up a cedar log with one of his tiny arms and throws it on the fire. I'm impressed at his accuracy considering how uselessly tiny his arms are.

"Good throw," I say.

"Thoreau?" he asks, then says, "No," pointing to his book, "that was Emerson."

I pause for a moment.

"I don't think that's right," I say.

The cedar log is burning, and the field is filled with a pleasant aroma.

"You look tired," says Rex as he motions to another (much smaller) recliner across from his on the other side of the fireplace. "Why don't you sit down and relax for a little bit?"

"Thanks," I say. "I've just been really stressed out lately. I've never been very good with winters."

"A dinosaur is what he thinks about all day long," says Rex, adjusting his bifocals as he reads from his book.

"I don't think that's right," I say.

It's interesting. People never missed dinosaurs until they realized that they were gone and they weren't coming back. At least spring is coming back. At least color would be coming back. At least I have a quiet moment to share with Rex in this field next to the sweet smell of burning cedar.

This seems much better than sitting at a fast food restaurant.

I look up at Rex. "You probably think our fast food places are absurd, don't you?"

Rex, whose tiny hand is now holding a Whopper, shakes his head. "These Whoppers are fucking great," he says and then throws the burger up in the air and catches it in his mouth.

"Nice throw," I say.

"I don't think that's right," he says and tosses me a Whopper.

"So, what do you think of the winter?" I ask, knowing full well that Rex had never had winter because he lived 200 million years ago during the Jurassic period when the climate was much hotter than it is now.

"The fire's nice," says Rex, as he tries to maneuver the book in his tiny arms to a place where one of the eyes on the side of his head can see it.

"But, what about all the cold and gray?"

"Well, nature always wears the colors of the spirit. Nature and books belong to the eyes that see them." The dinosaur stops for a moment to page through his book. "Also, nature hates calculators."

And the field is empty again. Perhaps Rex is right. Perhaps all I need to avoid seeing the gray is to look at things differently. Maybe rusty cars and salty roads can be as brilliant as a rainbow in the spring.

And actually, that grease smells pretty good. Maybe that dinosaur has the right idea. Maybe I should be a Whopper.

I know that Rex might say that Whoppers are only good food for dinosaurs.

But, I don't think that's right.

◆————————————————◆

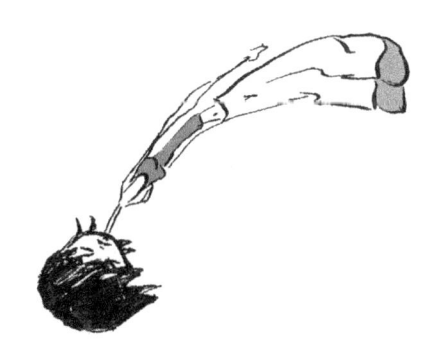

Measuring Light

by Elizabeth Varadan

Every day they walk back and forth between the missions. After breakfast they proceed toward Twelfth, along B Street, past the scrap metal yard, manufacturing plants, truck yards, before drifting away to other locations. Some sit on benches or on the grass at the Sixteenth Street park. Some walk south, past used-goods stores and warehouses, to panhandle or comb through trashcans.

Carl sits on a bench in the park.

At one o'clock they eat at long tables inside the Twelfth Street Mission. At four o'clock they line up outside the B Street Mission for soup served in plastic foam bowls along with a bagged sandwich. At six-thirty they return to the Bannon Street Mission to sign up again for the night's shelter. Carl doesn't need a watch for any of this. He pawned his anyway, long before he pawned his cameras. He moves in sync with the others, everyone drawn by invisible currents to converge at the right place at the right time. They walk in pairs or small groups. Or singly, in a separate space, like Carl. Some signal goes out; like migrating birds, they fall into place.

Birds in a line, a curve, a v-formation, wheeling in patterns against the backdrop of the sky. Scenes that used to take Carl's breath away. He never did capture an image that satisfied him. None that caught the wrench of heart he felt when he saw birds turn and soar in a group, then disappear into the distant sky. As the sun sinks lower, Carl walks along the bottom of the railroad yard, mumbling to himself, "Migration patterns."

The others don't know he's a photographer. They don't know his name. He likes it that way—there's no point in it; he's not one of them. This is temporary. As soon as he gets on his feet . . . .

Carl grunts. He is on his feet. He sets one foot down now, in a slow, prudent step, fearful of shuffling the way some of them do.

A car horn blasts. A silver Honda veers around him, the driver's face bunched in fury. Carl staggers back. Somehow he strayed out into the road. How did that happen? He licks his lips, and makes himself take a slow, steady breath, skirting closer to the grass, still trembling.

"That was a close one," he says aloud, and stops. He mustn't talk to himself. The others mutter like that. He's not one of them. Their faces wear blurred expressions, too, with rheumy eyes, stubbled chins, regretful mouths; faces interchangeable and anonymous. They frighten him. His hand goes instinctively to his own face. Perturbed, he takes it away. He thought he shaved this morning before breakfast.

No. That must have been yesterday.

He halts, breathing raggedly, blinking at a line of trees ahead, where the road bends to the right and leads to the shelter. Not even two blocks, but it feels farther than he once would have believed.

He can shave after he signs up for the bed, he decides. His razor is in his backpack, right next to his light meter. He carries his backpack everywhere, strapped to his back, so the others can't get it. They all carry things—worn satchels, shopping bags, shoeboxes. They wear recycled clothes, too—secondhand pants, ill-fitting shirts—as if they've all fallen out of the same basket of faded laundry. Carl keeps his own clothes on day and night, except when he showers. This morning he noticed egg stains on his shirt lapels and sweat blotches under his sleeves. His trousers are wrinkled. Soon he'll have to yield his clothes up, and they'll end up on someone else.

Fiercely he pulls his shoulders back, trying to straighten his spine. The effort makes him stumble, almost fall. He curses, then catches his balance, rounding the bend with slow, defeated steps.

*

Finished with soup and sandwiches, the men sit on the lawn outside the B Street Mission. Carl sits apart, against a post of the building, wearing someone else's clean khakis. Overhead, the afternoon sun is a pearlescent glare in a pale blue sky. Figures along the wall are splashed with light, hunched shoulders thrown in sad relief. Profiles of turning faces are rimmed with a faint sheen. Studying the luminous faces along the wall, Carl feels the stir of memory. Decisions about lenses and aperture settings float in his head. So much light to measure. His hands fumble with zipper of his backpack. After several tries, it opens. He takes out the rectangular black leather case and pulls out the light meter. The diffuser stares back at him, a wide, white, unblinking eye with hidden inner sensors. He presses the on switch, thinks a moment, and then rotates the small dial to 100 ASA. He sets the time for one sixtieth of a second and hesitates, running his tongue over his lower lip.

Outside shots are hard to do, people don't realize. He frowns. What he wants is reflected light—light rebounding off the surface it strikes, light the camera sees from a distance. He slides the diffuser to one side.

From a distance, memories rush up, reflect off one another, crash together, and angle off into fragments of scenes—wives, homes, the children he left behind (following in his father's footsteps like he swore he never would). Photography exhibits, write-ups and interviews,

all during the brief time when he could call himself a success. The ship he worked on when he joined the merchant marines. The many apartments his mother tried to turn into vocal studios. And a clear, sharp image of his sister, Rose, practicing piano scales when she was small, scowling near-sightedly at the music, her tongue moving against her lower lip almost in time to the metronome.

Sudden grief swells in him. The meter trembles in his hand. Carl pushes it into its leather case, puts the case back into the backpack, jerks the zipper doggedly until it closes, muzzling memory.

*

At night he doesn't sleep well, waking at odd times to see moonlight sifting around the edges of the window curtains. He dozes during the day. Everything is so turned around. Look at the way he has gotten old. He's only fifty, but his body is stiff and unyielding when he sits down or gets up. This morning the face looking back from the mirror was a thinner version of his grandfather's—the same puzzled blue eyes; same crinkled forehead, same hangdog mouth. And a shrunken down life. In his mind's eye, Carl sees the familiar huddled figure of his grandfather by the console, listening to Paul Harvey, the rest of the world tuned out.

When Carl boarded the merchant ship in '55, he had thought he was entering a panoramic life. He was only seventeen—he doctored the year on his birth certificate and his papers went through. Till then, everyone called him Sonny, a name he felt he had outgrown. He was a man, now, a merchant mariner about to see the world.

It was a short run, just to Venezuela. The pay was good, better than what he'd made in warehouses or washing dishes after he'd dropped out of high school. He had half his allotment check sent home and still he had money to spend. In Venezuela, he bought his mother a pair of gold earrings with zircon stones. He bought Rose a gold charm bracelet inlaid with blue enamel. One charm was a miniature whistle that actually made a tiny piping sound.

He loved the sea. He loved its range of moods, changeable like his own. It could be calm and smooth with a glassy sheen, or churning with waves, depending on the weather. Sometimes a ship would pass by, trailing a foamy wake. The brine smell. The endless horizon. The days with nothing in sight except schools of fish close to the water's surface. The color changed too: waves like chips from a coke bottle, ripples of jade green slate gray swells in a storm; and brilliant turquoise ruffles one clear day in October as they neared the coast of South America.

He couldn't keep up with the other men, though. Too dreamy. He didn't work fast enough in the engine room. On free time, he hung over the rail looking out at the sea instead of playing cards with the others. When the ship returned to San Francisco he was let go.

He remembers taking the bus to Lyon Street. Walking the two blocks from the park's panhandle, shivering against the damp cold in spite of his pea jacket, he'd wondered what he was going to tell his mother and sister. He rang the bell of the second story flat in the old Victorian, and a woman he'd never met opened the door. She wore a faded blue chenille robe. Her dark straggly hair hung to her shoulders. Two small boys and an older girl, about eight, crowded behind her. The girl stared gravely at him from big brown eyes that made Carl think of Rose at that age. His mother and Rose had moved. The woman didn't know where to.

That night Carl gave their presents to the cocktail waitress in a North Beach bar. He never tried to find them.

Strange, he thinks, lying in the darkened dorm. Strange that he would walk away like that. He could have looked for them—they were probably at his grandparents' house inLos Angeles, where his mother usually went when things didn't work out. What became of Rose? He wonders. At the time it seemed life was telling him to cut loose, stop being Sonny, go out on his own, spend his money on himself. It was so easy to slip away and disappear.

"I should have tried to find them," he mumbles under his breath. He can hear the other men breathing, ninety-two of them locked fast in their dreams. Or maybe they're awake, like him. He can hear his own breathing, the labored wheezing of an old man. Still, he won't talk to them. He's not one of them. He's just here till he gets his footing again.

He'll get a temporary job, buy some clothes, find a place to stay. He'll get his cameras out of hock, set up some exhibits; maybe even open a gallery again once he gets his photographs out of storage.

But no. He was behind in his payments. The storage company had sold all his boxes.

*

Noon. The shimmering sun showers heat on Carl as he makes his way to the end of the lunch line. Stories his grandfather told him about soup lines from the Depression come back to him. Even in his mother's gypsy wanderings, no one in Carl's family ever had to endure such things. Now here he is, showing up with doddering steps, as if keeping a missed appointment.

A few familiar faces greet him. He nods curtly, each time drawing back into himself to a safe distance. Some of the men mutter, but most are quiet, motionless, facing toward the front of the line—a pilgrimage for food, their expressions united by a common expectation. His own face must wear just such a look.

Foreheads and hair glisten, the countenances starkly lit from above, with charcoal shadows under brows, noses, and chins. The end of the line is in shade from a cluster of bushy trees between buildings. Carl's thumb and fingertips press restlessly as if holding the light meter.

Incident light, that's what he should use—light caused by the incidence of light falling on surfaces. The wonderful thing about the meter is that it can read the light falling in different places and take an average of the readings to determine the exposure.

The way all the events of your life can be averaged out. The way they all add up and lead somehow to a present you wouldn't have expected: The aperture narrows; the field deepens to an endless, bottomless gulf . . . .

Carl shuffles to the end of the line and turns his eyes numbly to the front. He can feel his lips making little pursing motions. Thoughts buzz at him, trying to take shape, a memory of himself explaining what he always felt was his masterpiece, Evening Approaches. There was no symbolism in it, he just liked sunsets. He'd always liked sunsets, though he felt he never did them well except that one time.

Ahead of him, an old man in a faded suit jacket jabs savagely at the ground with his cane. His own anxiety eddying, Carl clasps his hands to calm himself and waits for food. Back inside his own mind, he struggles to clarify Evening Approaches for his critics.

*

Whenever he walks to Fourteenth Street and one block over to A, he sees the ones with shopping carts. Some even have bicycles with bags hanging from the handles to collect what they scavenge in their rounds. Carl hasn't figured out where they sleep. They show up at the food lines, then go foraging for goods like entrepreneurs, no time to sit.

Half a block away, he sees three men and a woman consulting in the tunnel-like underpass of an immense concrete pipe, away from the harsh glint of the mid-morning sun. They separate. The woman strays out the other side of the tunnel and disappears. Two of the men push their bicycles in the direction of Fifteenth Street. The third, a wiry fellow with a scrubby brown beard, wheels his cart in Carl's direction. Under his red bandana, his burnt-out face suggests someone who has mixed too many drugs.

Carl's thoughts go to the woman. Most of the women find shelters and food lines of their own, but he encounters some of them in his wanderings, premature crones with uncombed hair, dresses that hang unevenly. They walk with raggedy gaits. They stir his sympathy. He always was too tenderhearted toward women. Never could resist them; that was what made so much trouble for him. Two wives and too many girlfriends, all hooking his ego, then turning bickering and blameful when things didn't go their way. Scenes overlay scenes, merge, vanish, and reappear—a clear picture of Eileen, his first wife, her bubble hairdo, her pink waitress uniform, the way she hovered over him at Poppy's Café, making a twenty-year-old boy feel like a somebody.

He was a stock boy at Harmon's Photography Supplies, Inc., on Mason Street in San Francisco. When they found out she was pregnant, Carl did the right thing. Regret makes him choke. What did he know about being a husband or father? For a little over two years they squabbled over everything, mostly about how to spend their meager earnings. They quarreled over the camera Carl bought, and Beth, one of the regular customers in the photography shop.

At first Carl just liked to talk to Beth about her photographs, how she got such dramatic effects in black and white. Photography had taken hold of him. Beth encouraged him to buy the camera, and pretty soon she was giving him lessons when her husband was out of town. One thing led to another, but he hadn't planned it that way. His son, Kenny was a year and a half; Eileen was six months pregnant again. Eileen divorced him, but Beth stayed with her husband. Carl was left with the burden of alimony and child support. And the camera.

He made a few payments, paid a few clumsy visits to his son, Eileen scowling at him as she burped Julie, or changed her diapers. One day he walked out of his job, bought a Greyhound bus ticket, and went to Los Angeles. Never sent another check. Never even wrote.

What became of them? Carl wonders. Did they manage to have a happy life? Do his children hate him the way he hated his father for leaving when he was a baby? He glowers at his younger, mortifying self; then is startled back when the man with the ravaged face draws his shopping cart right up to him and stops.

Carl stares in distaste at the deep-socketed eyes, the taut, lined skin, the gash-like mouth. No doubt this fellow is going to ask for money. He draws himself up to refuse. He doesn't believe in handouts. He's had to work for everything; so can this bum.

The man leans toward him with a confidential nod. "You might want to try Fifteenth Street."

To Carl the scene suspends endlessly in a void-like silence, a negative whose image isn't coming out right. At last he raises a quivering hand and runs it over his forehead, then his eyes, as if wiping away the moment. His hand drifts to his mouth, to his chin, where he finds bristly growth. He forgot to shave again; the knowledge cows him.

"I . . . , I'm . . . ." The words stick in his throat. The man lifts his brows, his mouth drawn in a quizzical line. "I'm not going to be here long," Carl manages. "This . . . ." He gestures at the empty truck lot, the concrete pipe tunnel, the intersection, the sidewalk where they stand. "This is just temporary." His mouth stumbles over the syllables of the last word.

The other man's lips curve in a downward smile. "Yeah. Me too. Just passing through, man. Just passing through." He rolls the cart past Carl and crosses the street, going toward Thirteenth. The red scarf becomes a blur. The rattling of the cart grows faint. Then fainter, until there is only heat and silence.

*

In the lunch line, a man with beetle brows, a recent arrival, stands behind Carl, clutching a plastic shopping bag. Carl has turned to ask him not to stand so close before seeing the food-stained tie, the rumpled clothes, the unshaven chin.

Under his gaze the man stares down at himself as if noticing his own ruined state for the first time. He looks up with a sneer. His eyes take in and give back the full picture of Carl, and Carl feels a dull ache spreading through his chest, rising up to his throat, seeping down to his belly. The man refuses to look away. Carl breaks the glance and turns to the long line of men ahead of them.

"Damn fools!" It wrenches out of him in a strangled cough, the words indistinguishable. But in his mind the words are loud. Loud!

Damn fools! I'm not one of you!

*

In the darkness of the dorm Carl lies thinking of Sandra, his second wife. She had that sunny disposition. It warmed him, thawed him out. They were in love. She believed in his

10

art. Her father put up money for the studio and gallery. Everything was going so well. They had the ranch house. Sandra kept the books, made appointments. All Carl had to do was take pictures, develop them, crop them, mat them, hang them. The happiest time in his life, before Pauline, that bitch, ruined things. Sued him for paternity. One slip! Till then, he'd only visited with her at her apartment, but she needed advice about her photography. He tried to guide her, show her. Timing and contrasts, the two keys. He never could explain any of it to Sandra. Never undo the hurt. Never make it up to their daughter. Grown now. Somewhere. So many girlfriends after that. Nothing the same again. Jobs at camera stores, developing film. Stock boy again.

His thoughts skitter back to the restless stirring of slumbering shapes around him. Why are there so many like himself? he wonders. Where did they all come from? He had once imagined derelicts to be an ill-favored few, a handful of bums on street corners, holding paper sacks with wine bottles inside. Now they seem everywhere, from every walk of life. He might have known any one of them in more favorable times. Cursed at crabgrass with them, when he had the ranch house. Mixed martinis with them at parties. Talked about art with them at receptions.

So many. Each of them someone. He reaches up to feel the backpack next to his head, his fingers tracing the shape of the black leather case inside.

Flash light. That's what he should use. Light that explodes when the flash goes off, distilling radiance into the air in a fraction of a second, making it easy to see the whole picture. His meter can measure that. It can measure every kind of light. Carl is seized with a sudden longing to get up and take the light meter around to each sleeping face, hold it close and take a reading. But, if they were to find him doing this, it would be hard to explain. They might take the light meter away from him. He lies still, folding his hands over his chest. After awhile, warmth glows under his hands, then under his rib cage, as if the box were inside him, measuring something small and luminous.

*

Carl sits in the shade under the sycamore tree, watching blades of grass catch the light from a slanting sun. It must be a little after four o'clock. The call to eat has gone out. Figures across the street rise and walk, like somnambulants, starting down C Street toward Twelfth. Others appear at the edge of the park from nowhere to join them. Eyes aslant, Carl watches them. Light splashes from above, haloing each face, each bent posture, as they fall into line.

Procession. The word rolls around in his mouth. Threads of light, too small to be seen, pull inside him, connecting him with them at a thousand touch-points. What difference does it make who any of them are? He rises, joints protesting, to take his place.

He fumbles for his light meter, taking it out, dropping his backpack on the sidewalk in his haste to catch up. He stumbles into the street, lifting the meter, turning it toward the moving promenade. A squeal of brakes is the only warning before Carl feels himself heaved into the air. The light meter soars out of his hand and he sees it rise in an arc, as if purposely flung high enough to catch the light that's falling everywhere.

◆——————————————————————◆

Short Term Memories

by Adam Sullivan

Scrubs was on. I had finished reading Jonathan Franzen's *The Corrections*, and was rewarding myself with junk food and sitcoms as I opened the day's mail—a magazine renewal form, a credit card statement, and a legal-sized package from my father that stood taller than my Big Mac.

My pediatrician had died, and his receptionist, a longtime family friend, had given my file to my parents. I don't know if this was protocol, or just small-town friendliness, but he passed it along to me in California, thinking I'd get a kick out of it. Every flu shot was in there, my annual bronchitis visits, the time I sat on a pencil and had a segment of graphite lodged in my butt cheek. And then I found a report from a doctor I couldn't remember, a psychologist.

Dear Dr. Carin,

Mrs. Sullivan asked me to do three observation grids on Adam in the classroom as Ms. Brezinski, his teacher, felt Adam was "bright" but an extreme underachiever. On reviewing the records, we found this has been a pattern since the 3rd grade, worsening each year.

My three 15 minute observations showed the following:

1. Often fails to finish things he starts.
2. Doesn't seem to be part of the class; as if he was somewhere else.
3. Has difficulty concentrating on school work as evidenced by staring in his lap during a movie on the civil war and during class discussions.
4. He spent most of his time starring downward at various objects (box, pencils, book) in his lap. The teacher said he's often reading in his lap while class is going on.

Adam appears lethargic (rubbing his eyes-yawning), a passive member of the class. Even when the class laughed at an amusing incident, he didn't seem to notice.

She had diagnosed me, in 1986, with Attention Deficit Disorder. It was late, but I phoned my parents, demanding an explanation. My father was groggy, but after a minute my mother remembered. "Oh yeah," she said. "We had you checked out for— you know—mental problems."

"Mental problems?"

"Yeah, they wanted to give you some drugs, but I just said 'forget it.'

"*Mental* problems?"

"It was fifteen years ago, Adam. Let it go."

But I couldn't. For weeks it kept me up at night. I employed the insomnia as Exhibit A in discrediting the psychologist's theory. If I did have A.D.D., wouldn't I have forgotten about that report in a matter of minutes? I was 25, beginning a career as an editor, so I took great pride in pointing out that the typewritten report had no fewer than three mistakes on the first page alone, proving I was not only smart, but petty. Self-doubt is a positively static condition, though, and a cursory look around the room began to paint a bigger picture. Books I'd never finished, a stack of thank-you cards I'd never written. I had a brief romantic notion to be a painter, the end-all result was a half finished canvas peeking out from behind the bookcase—two ghosts, snuggled up on a sofa, watching TV.

It took me nine years to earn a four year degree. "I moved around a lot" was my lame explanation to potential employers, and "I got screwed with transfer credits," was an equally lame one for my friends. But the truth was I just lost interest every few months. On the mantel of my grandmothers' house was a collection of mugs—each one adorned with the crest of a college or university that her grandchildren attended. There was Clark, from my sister,

Villanova from my cousin Michael, and on down the line. When she died, I had given her mugs from Dean, Uconn, Eastern Connecticut State, and San Diego City College. She may not have lived to see me graduate, but at least she thought of me as the smartest.

At night I tossed and turned. Uncertainty gnawed at my skull and I looked for evidence, one way or the other, the ghosts of embarrassments past showing me vignettes that made my skin crawl.

One night, on the verge of failing tenth grade, I was studying in the basement. I'd read a chapter, and within a few lines the words would blur and my mind would wander. I'd shake my head and try again. I tried reading aloud; figuring double-duty would help me retain the words. But hearing and listening exist on different planes. I sat there depressed, mind unable to conquer matter.

I could have walked upstairs and into the family room, where my parents were watching *Cheers* and *The Cosby Show*. I'd feel better the second I closed the book, but I couldn't. Sitting there, ashamed, was good for me—one of those moments that would be looked back on as pivotal, so I drank it all in—the treadmill, the old sofa, the muted sounds of sitcoms seeping through the ceiling, mocking me—canned laughter, applause.

A month later and I still couldn't stop thinking about the psychiatric diagnosis. A splinter, even a nasty one, stops hurting after a few days, but if left untreated, it can become infected. I went to the library to read up on A.D.D., albeit with low expectations. There are a hundred memoirs on Obsessive-Compulsive Disorder, because once you get the notion to sit down and write it, you can't stop until it's done. A book on A.D.D., however, would be next to impossible to finish. Completing a single chapter would be just shy of a miracle. And even if they were written, what publisher would think people with a dearth of attention would sit still long enough to read a book? But I was pleasantly surprised; there were a dozen books, both clinical and memoir. Most of the memoirs were about the various prescriptions that cured them, which is a pretty good indicator that the pills work.

Despite being called "One of the best-researched disorders in medicine" by the AMA, there isn't a hell of a lot that's actually known about A.D.D. For starters, there are a wide variety of factors that cause it, two particularly polarized examples are "Brain Defects" and "Giftedness." It's like saying you can get burned from both extreme heat as well as cold. I decided not to ask why my parents ruled out giftedness so quickly. A.D.D. because you're gifted, you can pass that off as the tortured artist angle. If you're A.D.D. because of a "Brain Defect," there's a different set of safety procedures and school buses involved.

I read that, rather than just living life completely out of focus, one of the traits was a tendency to "hyperfocus" on one thing, while tuning out everything else. I thought of the hundreds of hours spent perfecting skateboarding tricks, repeating them over and over, neglecting homework. The nights I stayed up until sunrise playing Nintendo, neglecting food. I looked up at the books, notebooks, pens, and laptop strewn out around me, blocking the entire aisle, forcing people to walk around.

I learned A.D.D. was first diagnosed over a hundred years ago, when it was called "Morbid Defeat Of Moral Control." Awesome name for a heavy metal album, not so awesome as a disease. It assumed several identities throughout the next 80 years—1968's "Hyperkinetic Reaction" being far and away the coolest—until 1980, when it became Attention Deficit Disorder. I turned five that year.

All things considered, I got off pretty lucky.

In the past, doctors tried to treat A.D.D. with everything short of exorcism, but in 1987 all they did was offer my mother some experimental pills, beta versions of Ritalin and Adderall.

In high school, I didn't drink or use drugs, identifying with a group of friends who labeled themselves "Straight-Edge." Were I to take amphetamines each morning, I'd have gone through high school with no friends whatsoever. This was also the time of my life that was spent polishing off a two-liter of Mountain Dew each day. We'd learn about irony in the coming year.

I read through half a dozen case studies, and several traits jumped out at me: poor handwriting, fidgety, impulsive, inability to focus. It's like reading a horoscope—you can apply any generic advice to your life and find a connection. It's dangerous to read symptoms first and then retrofit them to your life, but it was hard not to notice a pattern.

It wasn't so much that I had a disorder, but realizing that not everyone shared my problems made my blood freeze.

When I got home Ann was watching TV.

"Hey," I said. "I think I might have A.D.D."

"Yeah," she said, not looking up. "No shit."

Wait—it was *obvious*? I'd spent my life assuming everyone tuned out whenever someone spoke for too long. The world suddenly seemed so unfair. All my memories— blurry pictures, fragments of sound, a puzzle, forever missing pieces.

When someone has a debilitating condition or experience, it's only natural to wonder what it's like. It's generally considered rude to ask direct questions, but I think it's just as rude to feign disinterest. So I ask. "You were in an asylum for seven years? How's the food? Tell me *everything*."

If I met someone as impolite as myself, I'd have no problem answering their questions. But unfortunately, I can't explain what it's like, because I simply don't know what it's *not* like. I wasn't suddenly struck with the disorder in the middle of cracking the genome. It feels like I can't put together an eloquent thought. I *feel* them in there, though. Working one into conversation is impossible, but if I sit and edit and revise long enough, I can sometimes make a point. It can be frustrating, and before long I found myself considering a prescription.

"Well, you don't sleep. That's for sure." Josh was patiently answering all my questions..

"But what's it *like*?" I pressed for details as though Ritalin were some magical fairyland where you could read more than one chapter at a time.

He thought a minute before answering, and I envied his concentration. "Your drive to work is the same, but once you get there you can tell me how many blue cars you passed." I was enchanted. I instantly wanted to try it, not only for the attention span, but I desperately wanted to steal his analogy.

My brother-in-law gave me a couple pills in a jar. They were smaller than I thought they'd be. The jar sat on my desk for a few days, but I never took them. All the case studies I read listed the positive qualities found in A.D.D. patients— specifically creativity and enthusiasm, which was pretty much all I had for positive qualities. Without them, I'd never have painted ghosts watching TV—well, I wouldn't have started to paint them.

Giving my problem a name turned it into an excuse. Taking medication would become a crutch. Sooner or later I'd be one of those people who assumes bragging rights about a disorder. Once it's official you become an object of pity, which I'd quickly ruin by milking it. The pills became a symbol, and taking them was a tacit admission of defeat. I decided to continue taking pleasure in life's little victories—finishing a book, earning a diploma, two ghosts watching TV— maybe it would get easier to concentrate with practice and willpower.

I walked down the hall to my office to file the psychology report between my diploma and a few stories I'd gotten published. Peeking out from behind the bookcase, my ghosts stared at me, their eyes lifeless and unfinished, and in that moment I was reborn, my disorder temporarily cured by willpower and ignorance. I lay down some newspaper and took out my paintbrush, leaving the TV on for inspiration, its familiar sounds still begging me to return, but ultimately proud of me for resisting.

Canned laughter. Applause.

The Facts of the Case

By Neil Mathison

The evening her ex-husband phones, it's raining and she's under the weather from another round of Estriol. Linguine steams in the colander. She's dicing a clove of garlic. From her kitchen window – her "eagle's aerie" she calls it – she can see the harbor. Sometimes she sees real eagles too, gliding heavily over the water, dropping below the tops of the tallest firs. Or she watches the Washington State ferry nosing into its landing, its decks white and green and layered like a wedding cake.

Robert is calling from Pt. Barrow, in the far northwest corner of Alaska. "I'm driving down the Al-Can," he says. "Okay if I stop by?"

Static hisses through his words. She hasn't seen Robert in seventeen years. Still, the instant she hears his voice, warm and mellow and reminding her of chords he played on his acoustic guitar, she recalls their wedding more than thirty years ago – her rainbow dress, his white Nehru jacket, the cowry-shell necklace that hung from his neck, how fog reached under the Golden Gate Bridge, up into the park, enveloping the wedding party in icy arms.

She asks if he still ministers to Eskimos.

"Aleuts," he answers. "They've got it all – alcoholism, drugs, VD. A microcosm of the American millennium."

She remembers this tough-love talk, his disorganized idealism, the obsessive care he gave his collection of Dylan records; how she had to teach him to change the oil in his Volkswagen bus.

"I heard about your MS," he says. "Sorry."

"We live on an island," she answers. "You'd have to take the ferry."

"How's Richard?"

"There are only two ferries a day."

"I'll catch the morning boat."

When she cooks, especially lately, since the MS, she finds herself recalling random moments from her life: being tear-gassed with Abby Hoffman in '68, practicing law at Westinghouse, cycling through Tuscany with Richard on a tandem bike. She recalls her affairs – six premarital and one post – and how she won the women's squash championship at the San Jose Athletic Club. Sometimes the memories arrive unbidden, surprising her like the flavors in a well-simmered broth. Salt, slice, soak. *rijsttafel, gazpacho, zabaglione*. She cradles the phone against her shoulder. Robert's breath husks through the receiver: *in, out, in, out*. She tries to concentrate on her recipe: *three quarters cup of walnut oil, preferably French; a teaspoon of allspice; four cups of freshly grated Parmesan cheese*. Outside, a vine maple scrapes the windowpane like bone on a slate. *Two cups of walnuts, toasted*. When they first met she'd found Robert inspirational, then pedantic, finally oppressive. She wonders how much he has changed.

"Hello," he rasps through the phone. "You still there?"

"Okay. You can come."

Before he hangs up he tells her he's met a woman. "She's Catholic," he says. "We might get married."

These are the facts of her life.

She ran two marathons (New York, 1981 and Boston, 1983), married twice (Haight-Ashbury , 1970 and Palma, Majorca, 1985), chartered a sailboat in Turkey (1992). She became an accomplished chef. Now the smell of a food can make her nauseous. Collecting the mail leaves her breathless.

Since her diagnosis five months ago, her husband, Richard – West Point (1955), a New York Stock Exchange seat (1970-84), prostate cancer victim (remitted since 1993) – has become an expert on multiple sclerosis. There are new regimens, he insists, to arrest her disease: Avonex, Copaxone, Betaseron; acupuncture and vitamins. He urges her to try a vegetarian diet.

Lately, the smallest things – a magazine photograph, the aroma of ginger outside a Chinese restaurant, a Beetles song – will trigger a deluge of memories. She worries: will she have time to remember? She wonders: does it really matter if she remembers?

Consider the facts: she has lived a full life.

Consider the fact: she still wants to live her life.

She insists her doctor spare her no detail about her MS.

Dr. Baer tells her this: lesions are forming on your myelin, the protective sheath that surrounds the nerve fibers, on your optic and auditory nerves, on your spinal column, even in your brain. New, encouraging therapies exist. But each case is unique. We can't be certain what will work. The disease may remit and recur at unpredictable intervals. It can be slowed. But never fully arrested. You will someday likely suffer permanent weakness, someday possible paralysis, someday probable loss of eyesight and memory, someday a diminishing of your thought processes. It probably won't kill you.

My companion for life, she thinks.

The loss of her memories troubles her most. "You'll have to care for me like a baby," she tells Richard.

"Frankly my dear," he answers in his poor Rhett Butler imitation, "As long as you're with me, I don't give a damn."

"I'll be a vegetable."

"Then be an artichoke. I love artichokes."

She promises Richard that should her ex-husband Robert stay overnight, she'll mix Richard a pitcher of martinis, this despite her nagging Richard to cut back on martinis.

Richard sits in his big wingback chair, back straight like a cadet, his military bearing belying his gentleness. "I'll take mine shaken, not stirred," he says, affecting his even worse than Rhett James Bondish faux British accent. "With olives."

"But if he leaves without spending the night," she adds, "you make the martinis, mine with pearl onions, straight up."

"You don't like martinis," Richard says.

"But I like the onions," she answers. "And I like watching you make them."

The day Robert is due to arrive, she wanders through the house, straightening a picture frame here, placing cut daffodils on the kitchen counter, plumping the sofa pillows for the third time. She plans a Spanish dinner: *tapas*, gazpacho, paella. She has cooked the chicken, de-veined the shrimp, scrubbed the clams, sliced *chorizo*, peeled onions, checked that she has the right seasonings – saffron, garlic, fresh red peppers, paprika, and oregano. On the stove her broth simmers.

"Smells like heaven," Richard says, his golf bag swinging from his shoulder. "What is it?"

"Chicken stock. For paella."

"Cook it well. Life's too short for bad paella." He leans to kiss the nape of her neck. "I'm hitting the links."

"You'll miss Robert's arrival."

"I know."

"Coward!"

Richard waves cheerfully as he escapes out the door. "He's not my ex-husband."

Robert misses the morning ferry. When he finally arrives, he stands at the door, taller than she remembers, slim-hipped (still) and pony-tailed (as always), but his hair, once the color of acorns, has turned a rust-streaked gray. An amulet hangs from his neck: a leather pouch, a few owl feathers, the foot of an Arctic hare, all tied together with a doeskin thong. She leans to kiss his cheek and touches the amulet with her fingers. She's surprised at its softness, like Robert's skin as she remembers it on the inside of his thighs.

An Aleut dream catcher, he explains.

His car, a new Toyota, blocks the driveway. It's streaked with mud and filled with cross-country skis and backpacks and Primus cook stoves and cardboard boxes that overflow with clothing and magazines and dog-eared books. Robert never gives away books. Until this moment, she hasn't wanted him to stay. Now she tells him she'll make up the guest bed.

"You look terrific," he says.

She glances at her reflection in the hall mirror. She's still slender, although her chin, she thinks, is too small and her forehead too large. Her short hair remains black. *Black as raven's feathers*, Robert used to say. But now her face is drug-puffy from the Estriol and her eyes are ringed and hollow.

They sit at her kitchen table, next to the window where Robert can best see the harbor. He fingers a daffodil petal. "Nice."

"From the local greenhouse," she explains.

Neither has stayed in touch with shared old friends. Robert sips a glass of red wine. "Join me in a glass?" he says. "Red wine makes you live longer."

She sticks to water.

"So what's with your MS?" He screws up his face — a gesture intended, she supposes, to show concern.

She shrugs. "I try to ignore it."

"How like you." He shakes his head. "Always so tough."

"Let's talk about something else."

He tells her of his work in Alaska: stories about abused wives and abandoned children, ill-conceived government programs and unsympathetic authorities. Beneath each story lies a parable: the dignity of the underclass, the stupidity of bureaucrats. His anecdotes are the same as they were twenty years ago, set in Pt. Barrow instead of Oakland, told with dream catchers instead of street jive. But as he talks, she is surprised to discover how much she still feels the electricity of his persona. When he touches her shoulder to emphasize a point. When he grasps her hands to signal the profundity of one of his conclusions. His eyes, brown and sorrowful, seem as though they could bear all the suffering in the world. I'm being conned again, she thinks. But it's almost fun, being conned, at least if you're conned by Robert. There is something in it dangerous, beguiling, sexy. There's even a moment as they stand side-by-side at the sink — Robert has offered to peel the potatoes — when their hips touch, and she is tempted. What would it be like? What would it be like, she wonders, after so many years, to make love to Robert?

Later, while she prepares a spinach salad, Robert sits across the counter thumbing through photo albums she has forgotten to put away. The albums are of Richard and her, of their travels together. She has been studying them, hoping that if she commits the photos to memory, perhaps her past will slip more slowly from her mind.

"Where's this?" Richard asks after every few photos.

"Turkey," she answers. Or Sienna. Or Bora Bora. Or Hong Kong. Each photograph a memory: the azure Aegean; a cafe she and Richard found just off the *Piazza del Campo*; the voluble little monk they met on a Wanchai tram; the photos fix the track of her life.

"I need a favor," Robert says suddenly.

"What's that?"

"I want an annulment."

She lays the leaf she's been washing on the butcher-block board, wipes her hands on her jeans, turns off the faucet.

"We're already divorced," she says. "Or did I miss something?"

He pulls a blossom from one of the daffodils and holds the petal up to his eye. "I told you. I'm thinking of getting married. She's Catholic."

"You can't annul what doesn't exist."

"We can." He stares at her earnestly, as if he was about to deliver the punch line to one of his parables. "We fill out a few forms. Answer a questionnaire. As long as we agree to the facts – and neither of us contests it – the Church will grant our request."

"The fact is we were married."

"Only seven months." He rolls the daffodil petal into a tiny tube.

"As I recall we consummated the marriage – or don't you remember?"

"Of course I remember." He places his fingers to his forehead, what he does when he meditates, his eyes closed, his lips pressed together. She'd forgotten how much this irritated her, as if he is speaking over her head, addressing a plane that's beyond her understanding. "It's a matter of intent."

"For having no intent, we sure screwed each other's brains out."

"You're being difficult."

Her hand grips the edge of the sink; she feels the smooth coldness of the metal under her fingers like a stethoscope or a scalpel. "I don't think so."

"For Christ's sake!" Robert crumples the blossom into a tiny yellow knot. "We were kids."

"We were married. You can't wish it away."

"I've never asked you for anything."

"You asked me for a divorce." She remembers how he'd already packed his Volkswagen bus, how he wrote her a month later from Monument Valley that he was sharing a hogan with a Navajo girl. *I'm growing in a different direction*, his letter had said.

"Just look at the questionnaire." He extends his hand toward her clutching the sheaf of limp papers. "How can it matter?" He can't quite hide his anger. She can see it in the set of his jaw.

She looks past him through the kitchen window. The bare maple limbs frame the harbor. The water's surface is mirror-still.

Why *does* it matter?

Consider: in multiple sclerosis, her body will progressively fail. She will grow deaf, lose her sense of touch, her sight, her ability to walk, to speak, to feed herself, to use the toilet on her own. She will become a prisoner in her body, as her body collapses into what will be her ultimate solitary confinement.

Consider: without her history, who will she be?

"No," she says.

He turns away, staring out the window. "You haven't changed. You're still a hard-hearted bitch."

"Get out."

His gaze snaps back from the window. She watches surprise flash across his face.

"I'm sorry." He attempts a smile. He brushes his fingertips across her hip. "That was inappropriate."

She moves closer to the sink, beyond the reach of his hand. She picks up her knife and begins scribing a spinach leaf into tiny triangles.

His elbows rest on the counter. He folds his hands prayerfully. The annulment questionnaire still dangles from his fingers. "This means a lot to me." His eyes are child-wide. He wears his sincere face, a face that once always persuaded her.

"What it means to you," she says. She has carved the spinach triangles smaller and smaller, until they're little more than green stain on the cutting board. "Everything always for you."

"What does *that* mean?"

"*You* demanded a divorce. *We* never even discussed it."

"Let's discuss it now."

"Oh Jesus!" She tosses the knife in the sink. It clatters into the garbage disposal. "You use people. You even use your Aleuts to justify how compassionate you are."

"Look," he says, "the marriage was a mistake." His hands grip the counter as if he's trying to steer the conversation in another direction.

"You're damned right it was a mistake."

"So why does it matter? An annulment or a divorce? Who cares?"

"It wasn't an annulment. We divorced. Those are the facts." She takes a deep breath. "I'm not certain you'll understand this." She brushes an imaginary hair from her forehead. "If you pretend a thing that's happened didn't happen, you change who you are– you devalue yourself."

With sudden, ecstatic clarity she's certain this is true.

He shakes his head. "After all these years, you still want to hurt me."

"This has surprisingly little to do with you," she says.

But she wonders: Is *that* true?

"Isn't there anything I can do?"

"Talk to your fiancée. Persuade her."

He rises slowly to his feet still clutching the papers in one hand, fingering his dream catcher with the other. "I'll sleep in the car." he says. He tosses the questionnaire on the countertop. The pages flutter to the floor like little white doves, weightless and insubstantial. "I'm not leaving until we discuss this calmly."

"Suit yourself."

He turns abruptly and glides to the front door. Like an athlete or a dancer. Like water in a stream. Like silk in a breeze. She has always loved the way he moves. "Get a life," he calls out as he slams the door behind him.

I have a life, she thinks. I've always had one.

When Richard returns home, she's sitting at the kitchen table, staring at their photo album. Richard leans his golf bag against the table. "Where is he?"

"In his Toyota."

For fifteen minutes she has lingered over one picture, in Mallorca, in 1985. Richard and she have just gotten married. They are standing on the steps of the Palma City Hall, she in a cream muslin suit, he a wrinkled navy blazer. He holds her bouquet in front of his mouth, pretending to eat the flowers.

"He won't leave until I agree to an annulment."

"A little late for that."

"He says I'm being a hard-hearted bitch."

Richard shrugs. "I'll talk to him." He swings the refrigerator door open and removes a six-pack of microbrews. He leans close to her. She can feel the warmth of his breath against her ear, smells its fragrance of cinnamon and cloves. "You're probably being hard-hearted," he whispers, "but you're my kind of bitch."

While he's gone all she can think of are spices. Richard insists on alphabetizing them in their cabinet drawer. *Allspice, basil, bay; cardamom, chervil, chili; chive, cinnamon, cloves, and coriander.* By the time she reaches *nutmeg,* she can't recall what comes next. Perhaps she *is* being too hard. Maybe she *should* agree to the annulment. But she's afraid. Consider: if she lets even one fact go, she might lose them all.

When Richard walks into the kitchen he's whistling. He pretends to click his heels. He salutes. "Mission accomplished."

"He's leaving?"

"I told him he could keep the six-pack."

"He left because you gave him beer?"

"I told him I'd have a heart-to-heart talk with you."

She stiffens. "I don't want to discuss this..."

"OK." He lifts the lid on the saffron rice. "The matter's closed. When's dinner?"

"He's really gone?"

"Gone with the wind."

The aroma of paella fills the kitchen, steamy with garlic and oregano. For the first time in days, at least since her ex-husband's phone call, perhaps since her diagnosis with MS, she relaxes, suffused within the kitchen's warmth, by Richard's presence, feeling safe in a manner she doesn't quite understand. She can barely keep her eyes open – a symptom of the Estriol is it? The fingers of her left hand are numb. Nothing, she thinks, nothing has really changed. But still, despite the inevitability of her disease, despite the hard, cold weight of her MS, she senses danger averted, self preserved, a spirit lifting like the eagles she watches lift on the wind. What else is there to preserve?

"I'll have my Martini dry," she says, "straight up, don't forget the onions."

Wordplay✗Wordplay

The Cliché of an Alcoholic Parent

It isn't until you stop

watching the pot

that it decides to boil

over. Hot liquid spills and

falls to the floor.

A tree alone in the forest

cuts itself down,

no one hears it.

Yet tree sap remains

after the body has been

removed, rinsed and

reduced to pulp.

Ryan Martinez

Strawberry-Glazed-Chocolate-Cake-Boys

By Mario Leal

There was no definitive moment when I first knew, no sudden revelation like reading a quote from a great thinker and being baffled by the truth. There was always just something there, an awareness of things. The natural curiosity that makes you look over when standing at urinals in elementary school, or the way you empathize with the longing of teenage girls strung-out on neurosis and chocolate.

People ask when I first knew I was gay. Personally, the question seems queer, so I just ask when they first knew they were straight. Growing up, I did not know what gay was. Things like this are not discussed around dinner tables in the Valley. Gay is a word far removed from the lexicon of Texan border towns, and only seems to rear its ugly head when shouted as insults on schoolyards and as the butt of jokes.

I can remember a moment when I was around nine or ten, the stage where the pink elephant entered the room. I was walking from the car carrying my books, cradling them against my waist the way I was apparently not supposed to hold them. Two of my aunts were murmuring. They looked like a gaggle of gossipy geese from an animated film, with their children huddled around them,. They had judgmental looks painted on their faces. Whether I didn't hear or whether I chose to forget I cannot tell, but I knew they were talking about me.

"Boys don't do that. You wanna be a girl?" one of them said to me.

My ears flushed from the wound, and I still sometimes feel awkward walking with things in my arms. Stand up straight seems like a pun now.

There was another incident in Junior High. My mother and I were driving back from the store; it was the middle of the night.

"You do like girls don't you?" she asked.

As if maybe this time when she asked, with urgency and self-defeated hope in her voice, the answer would be different. As if there was a choice. As if there was some sort of decision to be made.

We were talking about religion. She said I was a preteen and when I turned thirteen God would start to judge me for my sins. As if it's suddenly your birthday and you're adult enough to smoke and get married and know what Life is all about; like someone turned on an imaginary switch in your head. I don't know where she gets these facts from. Maybe that's why I don't believe in God; I've never cared for ultimatums.

What does a child say to such a question? I didn't know what to say, so I just said yes. The image of a scrawny twelve year old pitted against pulpits. Against tradition. Against himself. Against the weight of the world. All this while buckled up in the front seat of some blue station wagon driving home from Walmart.

There are countless incidents. A life pocked with blemishes, each one still sensitive to the touch. Personal reflections and reasons to deny the existence of Lisa Frank school supplies. Sideways glances and knowing I'm the topic of discussion.

Being gay isn't something that happens overnight. It isn't checking a sexual orientation box on my Myspace and switching it back the next day. It's a long drawn out process of trial and error, testing limits and mannerisms and characteristics. It's playing dress-up in boys' clothes when everyone is calling you a girl. Growing up through realizations and brutal truths. Falling on playgrounds at the hands of

21

other boys and gossiping with the girls. It's facing yourself.

A moral quandary brought this home for me, when I worked for the Boys and Girls Club. I was a recent hire, maybe about three weeks into the job. Already outed as the "artsy" person trying to teach over forty delinquent, underprivileged students photography with one camera.

Of over a hundred students, there were only two who were, obviously, destined to be gay. One of these boys walked in while I was speaking to one of my supervisors, a coach. The coach was in the kitchen, cooking and washing dishes with some students. The boy stood there as we continued our conversation, awkward. Glasses, crooked teeth, chubby. The kid was already a walking insult.

When we finished talking and I started to walk out, the coach asked the boy how his "girlfriends" were. His dark-skinned, pudgy thirteen-year-old body flushed and became rosy. It reminded me of strawberry glaze on chocolate cake. I froze, numbed by shock, a surge of empathy and rage writhing through my body. I didn't know what to say. I couldn't even address it. The boy was standing right there. If anyone said anything, I knew he would crumble.

He somehow got quieter, even though he wasn't speaking. As if something deep inside him suddenly went silent. Like watching a house grow dark, nothing stirring. He looked down and pushed back the glasses sliding down his sweaty nose.

The coach realized what he said and blushed at me. I walked away. The boy asked the coach for the keys to get the mop and broom. It was clean-up time.

My mind raced that night with everything that was my life and probably the boy's life too. Of coaches. Of silence. Of feeling absolutely isolated by a comment or sideways glance. Of

dancing at clubs. Of playing with other boys. Of having to actively seek out a community because no one is really raised in it, or educated in it. Of facing walls. Of broken souls. Of fighting. Of dying. Of finding brothers and sisters. Of finding yourself.

I felt ashamed for not being stronger then and now and probably tomorrow. The coach avoided me as much as he could after that. We fell into absurdist mannerisms of ducking and hiding like those in a farce. When I quit a few weeks later I told them the job was taxing me and my grades were suffering. I never mentioned or told anyone about the incident. I assuage my guilt with the image of him washing dishes and cooking. Who's the emasculated one now?

Knowing that you're gay grows and swells. It comes in waves, ebbing and flowing with progress and everyday failures. I've always known I was gay. One day it was a curiosity. Next it was a word. And then a label. And then maybe one day it's part of an identity, or maybe something in between, or maybe it doesn't matter at all?

The road to your identity, to you, to your life, is not easy. For anyone. Not for coaches, or aunts, or mothers or strawberry-glazed-chocolate-cake-boys. Everyone will hit a pothole. Everyone will have to take a detour. No one is really going to end up who they thought they would be. Or who their parents thought they'd be.

Although I've always known in one way or another, facing it is something totally different. There is no one day that you know you're gay. There is only the day when you realize you can't lie about it anymore. When the pink elephant starts to make such scandal, propriety has flown the coop.

The question should not be, "When did you realize you were gay?"

The question is, "When did you accept it?"

Pricks

by Rick Monaco

"You ever get that thing looked at?"

Myron stared accusingly, beady black eyes narrowing as he focused on Carl's face. He rubbed a hand over his closely-cropped, prematurely white hair and knitted his dark eyebrows in feigned concern. They were two of three customers at the Broken Ship, a nondescript bar they had favored throughout their thirties. While not particularly striking, the small mole at the base of Carl's nose was enough to get Myron's blood pumping.

Carl mimicked Myron's motion, staring behind the bar at the mirror and feeling his own equally short, black hair, breathing slowly through flared nostrils. "Is that a cable-knit sweater she's wearing?" he said, glancing at the bartender at the far end of the room. It had been snowing all day in Brooklyn. A few stools down, a man in a Carhartt jacket and baseball cap nursed an after-work Budweiser .

"My Uncle Phil had a mole," Myron continued. "For years they thought it was nothing, then one day my aunt made him get it checked out..."

They'd known each other since high school - Myron a graduate and Carl a drop-out - and were both raised by largely absent fathers. Myron's logged millions of business travel miles while extending a coke habit into his sixties, and Carl's died shortly after Carl turned sixteen.

"What's your problem, anyway?" Carl finally responded. "It's a small mole. Benign. A goddamn beauty mark, ok?"

"Sorry," Myron said, grinning slightly. "Skin cancer is a frequent concern among those of Nordic descent. It's a common worry among my people."

"Your people?" Carl asked, perking up a bit. "You mean the Assholes?"

Outside the Broken Ship snow continued to fall. It had been coming down for two days and started sticking that morning. The first day presented a nightmare commute with cars sliding in all directions. Now the schools were closed and most locals stayed at home. A few all-wheel drive Manhattan cabs passed quietly on the white, flake-softened street. The front window of the bar was fogged and you could just make out the yellow glow of the sign on the Chinese takeout place directly opposite.

"Do you and Catherine eat out much?" Myron asked, switching gears.

"No, we prefer eating in," Carl answered, emotionless, his jaw now clenched.

"A lot of fine restaurants in Williamsburg," Myron persisted. "I'd think the curiosity would get the better of you."

Carl had met Catherine in high school. She was sweet-faced but plain and had put on fifty pounds in the years since graduation. She had also developed an agoraphobic condition severely limiting the times she left home outside of work. Myron was acutely aware of each of these facts and that Carl shielded her from interacting with him - it had been ten years since Myron had seen Catherine. Carl's social life was divided in two separate parts; the time he spent alone with Catherine, and a weekly round of beers with Myron. Catherine didn't question the time he was away from her or the way he spoke of it in elevated terms when he came home. He made it sound like they were two men blowing off steam, the way men sometimes need to do.

Carl waited a few beats before opening his mouth again. He raised his glass but didn't take a drink, putting it down and saying nothing.

"Peter Luger's is over there," Myron continued. "If you wanted to keep it old school, I mean. A bit pricey but not out of your range, and the steaks are supposed to be the best in New York. Catherine isn't vegetarian, is she?"

"No, she's not a vegetarian." Carl glanced down distractedly at his shoulder, as though there were something there he might brush off.

A loud crash caused them to both turn their heads abruptly. The man in the Carhartt jacket was sprawled on the floor ass-first, his bar stool having shot out from underneath him. His ball cap landed a few feet away revealing a mostly bald head, and the overturned stool continued to rock on its side next to him.

Cable Knit abandoned her Cosmopolitan magazine at the far end of the bar, rushing over with concern. The man regrouped quickly, embarrassed but not injured. He replaced his cap and righted his seat, retrieved the bottle, then beat a hasty retreat out the door. The bartender wiped the condensation away and watched him through window, making sure he remained on his feet. She cleared his beer and wiped the bar.

"Whatever he was drinking!" Myron said, grinning with forced confidence and pointing to the empty glasses in front of them. She stared blankly, refilling their pint glasses and not bothering to take their money, then returned quickly to her magazine at the other end.

"Lesbian?" Myron asked Carl half-heartedly, staring at the rising carbonated bubbles in his freshly-tapped pint. Carl played with his coaster and said nothing.

***

"So I said 'Who's that, the Assholes?'"

Carl was beaming proudly, recounting his exchange with Myron for Catherine. She smiled sympathetically, sitting next to him on the couch eating pistachio nuts.

"Did he respond?"

"I think one of his eyebrows moved. That's the equivalent of having a heart attack for Myron."

They'd lived in New York for nine years, moving there in December of 2001. For Carl it represented complete affirmation of Catherine's commitment to him, her being

willing to take this chance and leave the familiarity of their home. For her it seemed an opportunity to confront her fears, moving this distance at this particular time. He told her it would be a series of self-contained steps, all limited to safely enclosed spaces, and that he'd be with her all the way. She was skeptical of his motivation - altruistic ideas of reconnecting with humanity in the wake of a disaster. What did he know of New York outside of a handful of trips to visit Myron? Still, it went surprisingly well at first. Her job in California allowed for a transfer to the New York office which, in turn, allowed for her working mostly from home. The largest single move she'd ever made to confront her agoraphobia resulted, ironically, in further cementing the condition.

"It's kind of nice out there," Carl said. "The snow quiets things down. Maybe tomorrow we could visit that record store off of Bedford .. I mean if you're up for it."

She smiled uneasily. "I'm not a total basket case, you know. Of course we'll go. After breakfast." They hadn't been out for several weekends, and the idea pleased him.

Carl had not fared so well in New York initially. He was fired from his first job at a literary agency before making it past the trial period. He was apprehensive of his boss, a well-manicured Ivy League sort only slightly older than him with a penchant for using the word largess. Carl's phone skills were lacking, and he alienated himself by setting off an office alarm repeatedly. Things picked up when he landed his second gig, a secretarial job at a financial firm on Lexington. He grew comfortable there and enjoyed feeling like a working part of the big city. But about three months in something happened. He was walking purposefully up Broadway near 23rd one afternoon when a young guy wearing an iPod and approaching in the opposite direction dropped his sunglasses. Carl touched the man's shoulder to alert him and without hesitation the guy clocked him -

one good shot to the eye - and kept walking. The incident marred Carl's early experiences in the city. There were times, even now, where he'd catch his reflection in the mirror and be certain he could still make out the shiner.

He got up from the couch and looked at the drifts accumulating on the window sill. "Doesn't look like it's letting up," he observed. She got up too, and they stood together watching the street from their third floor vantage.

***

Carl woke early Saturday, not disturbing Catherine and getting the Times from the bodega next door. There was an article in the music section about some Brad Mehldau sessions that were to be released on vinyl. He prided himself a jazz fan and Mehldau was his favorite pianist. Carl perused his neatly arranged collection of LPs - more than five hundred, filed alphabetically by artist. He didn't play them much anymore - didn't listen to music like he used to, and when he did it was more often a CD. But he liked knowing that they were there and enjoyed having his old, heavy Marantz turntable operable and on display. He pulled out his original Riverside recording of Art Blakey's Caravan and looked at the cover without removing it from the plastic sleeve. It still had the sticker from Amoeba Music on Sunset in Los Angeles. Myron was with him that day and had accused him of making a "vanity" purchase.

He readied the kitchen for breakfast so he could finish when he heard Catherine wake. Water was set to a low boil with eggs nearby for poaching, bread was in the toaster ready to be submerged, and bacon sizzled quietly in a heavy skillet, its aroma slowly circulating the three-room apartment. There was a slight squeak of bed springs from the next room and he waited to hear the rollers on the closet door as she fetched her robe before setting the toaster and cracking the eggs. She walked in

tying her hair back in a scrunchy just as they hit the simmering water.

"Morning, Doctor Breakfast."

"I've started using a small splash of vinegar in the water," he said. "It keeps the whites from separating."

"Sounds suspiciously racist."

Some of their best banter was at this time of day, when things still held promise and seemed new. He thought she looked good before getting ready, the opposite of some women who would fear being seen without makeup. He was fiercely protective of her, in what he imagined was a well-concealed manner. But she knew, and thought it both endearing and unnecessary. He placed their plates on the small kitchen table and poured coffee from a French press, a device he'd deemed superior after years of toying with percolators and Italian espresso makers.

They walked to the record store after breakfast, below a resilient winter sun dodging high clouds. It had stopped snowing but small crystals whipped by a strong intermittent wind sparkled in the cold air in front of them. Carl wore the new expensive leather gloves she'd got him for Christmas and she her new puffy-jacket with the fakefur-lined hood. They didn't speak, both conscious that she was 'out' and that it was the rare exception. Whatever he might say would seem forced, but eventually the silence felt equally so. "Funny how it gets even colder when the snow stops coming down," he said. And that was it until they got inside the record store.

Roundhouse Records was a favorite spot for Carl to stop and browse on his way home from work. It was a failing business in his estimation - not enough sales to stay open, but remaining afloat by virtue of the owner's cash infusions. He'd talked jazz with the guy while perusing the impressive selection of vinyl. Carl liked to take the conversation to a point that established his knowledge of the genre, and then shut up to underline the fact that he wasn't one of those boors going on exhaustively, regurgitating something he'd read in the Times the week before. A small bell jingled above the door when he and Catherine entered, another of the store's many touches that he thought 'respectable'.

No other customers were in the shop and after ten minutes of aimless wandering they both settled near the back by the bargains section. She was aware of him silently gauging her comfort, and it made her self-conscious. He grabbed one of two copies of Elton John's Greatest Hits, instantly recognizable by the cover featuring the star decked out in an all-white suit, over-sized sunglasses, and matching white fedora.

"My mom had this on eight track when I was little," he said. "It's one of my earliest musical memories .. her playing the shit out of 'Bennie and the Jets' on the cheap Radio Shack console in the kitchen."

Catherine picked up the other copy. "1974 - I wasn't even born yet."

The small bell on the door jingled again and two more customers entered. Carl felt the hot prickle of blood rush to his face as a sense of near-panic overtook him. "Oh fuck," he said pointedly, instinctively raising the LP to block his head.

She did the same, mimicking his action. "Is that Myron?" she whispered.

"Who else?" he said, holding the record rigidly in place. "And Andy Bresnick." He closed his eyes tightly for a moment, thinking. "Don't say anything," he told her, "and do exactly as I do."

They side stepped along the far wall, holding the Elton John albums to their heads with the cover facing outward - two furtive Captain Fantastics beating an awkward retreat. He turned his back to Myron near the front and put the album down atop a stack of Onion newspapers, holding the door open and

gesturing pointedly for her to do the same. Carl took her hand and hurried her along the sidewalk. About half a block down they could hear Myron's voice calling in exaggerated fashion from behind.

"Carl?! .. Carl?!! .. Is that YOU??"

Myron didn't follow, having too much fun seeing them pick up the pace each time he yelled. He kept it up until they turned a corner two blocks down, then stepped back in the record shop, smiling.

***

It was two weeks before they met again for beers at the Broken Ship. It hadn't snowed in that time but stayed cold. Icy, exhaust-marred chunks plowed from the street remained firmly in place on the edge of the sidewalk. It was just past seven and they sat at their normal post at the end of the bar while four younger guys shot pool and played Johnny Cash on the jukebox. Myron held off on the subject of having spotted Carl at the record store until they were on their second beer.

"Say..." he said in droll fashion, taking his time to look up and catch Carl's reaction before continuing. "Was that you I saw at Roundhouse Records the other weekend, hurrying out of the place?"

Carl chose not to take the bait, knowing it was futile. "What's with the Johnny Cash revival and these twenty-somethings?" he asked, looking down at the four guys around the pool table. "You'd think he never made a recording that wasn't produced by Rick Rubin. And when they do play something old it's always self-consciously hip, like that live 'Cocaine Blues' track."

"I could have sworn it was you," Myron went on. "I was in there with Bresnick and I said 'Hey, that's Carl' as these two people hurried out the door."

"Nope. Wasn't me."

"Yeah, yeah .. the guy even had your same gait. You know, that funny way of half-jogging

26

with elbows out to the sides? Except he was holding on to a woman with his other hand. I thought it might be Catherine at first but she looked a little too large in the caboose."

Carl stared silently at him, his eyes suggesting that Myron might not want to push it any further.

"You're sure that wasn't you? Your secret is safe with me if you've got a little plus-sized action going on the side."

Carl held his stare while taking a swig from his beer. "How is Bresnick?" he asked seriously, his eyes retaining the same glare of obvious displeasure.

"Andy?" Myron said, sensing he'd milked about as much as he was going to get out of this one. "Guy's the same. What I wouldn't do to have his problems. Fucking life of Bresnick. He doesn't even work anymore."

"He quit his job?"

"If you want to call it that. He didn't need the money anyway. It isn't a job when you can just decide 'fuck it' and leave without consequence."

"It isn't like you're heading up Homeland Security," Carl said, watching Myron for signs of an effective strike. "You work at Whole Foods."

"There's just something that isn't normal," Myron went on, "about a guy that age .. our age .. who isn't working."

Carl grinned, happy to be focusing on someone else. "It's been a long while since I've seen him," he said. "I'm going to call him. Seriously .. next week. The years are going by too fast."

"Years are like expendable cash for losers," Myron said, suddenly dejected and seemingly angry. "Only it's universal and we're all rich at twenty. Say we've got twenty bucks without putting a value on the dollar. That's a buck a year to spend before we hit middle age and the long, dark tunnel."

"Kind of bleak," Carl said. "What if you've got money, like Andy?"

"You're not listening," Myron said, glancing angrily over at the young guys still playing Johnny Cash. "He may be wealthy but he only gets twenty bucks like the rest of us. You can't buy your way out of it. He's a loser."

***

Bresnick lived in Manhattan, north of Houston Street in a large loft with seventeen foot ceilings. He'd been a pitcher for his high school and junior college baseball teams, but in recent years his body had gone a bit soft with inactivity and approaching middle age. His hair was blond and thin and he had brown eyes that appeared to well up without instigation. He had worked at a cafe in the West Village for ten years. Pay day often fell on his day off and he puzzled the boss by not having his checks automatically deposited and frequently forgetting to pick them up. One time when he asked for his check a week late, she inquired jokingly if he was 'independently wealthy.'

Bresnick's uncle, who taught him to play baseball, had been with the Hansen Natural Beverages company since shortly after its beginnings in Southern California, and acquired a good deal of stock after it went public. He left it all to Andy when he died in 1997, and Andy cashed out ten years later, retaining a hefty sum to invest conservatively after paying the capital gains taxes. The windfall left him estranged from the rest of his family, who received only token amounts. A rift already in place with his father, a wealthy businessman himself, was solidified by Andy's inheritance.

It was Tuesday night when Carl took the subway into the city and stopped by Bresnick's loft. The break from his entrenched routine of work, home, and beers with Myron invigorated him, and there was a bounce to his step as he walked down Great Jones Street. Andy buzzed him in and Carl took the lift up - a modified freight elevator officially canceling the designation of 'walk up' and adding substantial value to the building's upper units. Andy's was on the top floor. Carl had to check himself to not appear overly-impressed when he walked in. The door was open and Andy was catering to a large pile of clothes by an expensive looking washer and dryer setup.

"There he is!" Carl said grandly as Andy looked up and managed a grin. "Refreshing to know that even the greats can't escape the task of laundry."

Andy asked Carl to get them both a beer from the fridge as he continued folding clothes. Carl sized the place up. It was sparsely decorated with a few large paintings and a big flat screen on one wall. The front of the loft was all windows extending up almost to the ceiling.

"Goes up a long way in here," Carl observed, looking upward. "Must cost a fortune to keep this place cool in the summer." Andy raised his eyebrows, looking up from folding the last few shirts, but said nothing. Carl walked over to the windows and looked down. He had an odd sense of seeing the city for the first time.

"I don't mind saying it," he commented, taking a drink from his cold beer, "this is one hell of a place." Still, Andy said nothing. "Do you know the story of Great Jones Street? The guy who owned the property deeded the site to the city under the stipulation that they name it after him. Except there was already a Jones Street, so he insisted that they call it Great Jones."

"Never heard that," Andy said, looking up from the completed stack of folded laundry.

"Maybe if the building's here in another hundred years, some schmuck like me will be looking down on Great Bresnick Street," Carl said, watching Andy for a reaction that never came. He switched his approach back to sincerity. "Seriously, this is a nice setup. You're doing okay for yourself, old boy."

"I like the washer and dryer," Andy said. "It gets tiring lugging your clothes out to a laundromat every few weeks." He paused before continuing. "It doesn't make sense," he said.

"Carrying laundry around?"

"No .. Great Bresnick. There is no other Bresnick Street in the city, so why would they call it 'Great Bresnick'?"

"Oh ... yeah, right," Carl said, finishing his beer and holding it up. "How about we get another one somewhere local?"

Andy's 'local' was a few blocks down on Bowery, a dingy spot that hadn't changed with the gentrifying waves. They did a good business on the weekends with kids looking to 'keep it real' but Andy stuck to the sparsely populated mid-week scene. Carl insisted on buying the rounds. He had a good buzz going four or five beers in and was speaking in animated fashion by the glow of the small red Tiki lamps on the bar.

"So I said to him, 'It isn't like you're heading up Homeland Security for crying out loud .. you work for Whole Foods!'"

"Myron said I'm a loser?" Andy asked in matter-of-fact fashion, peeling the label on his Heineken.

"Everybody's a loser in that guy's goddamn world," Carl said, encouraged that Andy seemed to be paying attention. "Yeah, you're a loser according to Myron. 'Andy may be wealthy, but he's a loser.' I think those were his words. Sometimes I question why I hang out with the guy."

Andy ordered another beer and Carl pushed his pile of cash toward the bartender, insisting that he keep paying. "We saw you in that record store the other day," Andy said. "You were with your wife."

"That wasn't me."

***

Winter hung tough through March with a couple of late-season blizzards assuring no new growth on the trees. Catherine and Carl stayed home, watching television and playing a lot of

Scrabble. He took to sipping single malt whisky at night after a work colleague gifted him a bottle of Oban for covering his job while on vacation. Myron and Carl neglected their usual weekly get-togethers for more than a month, trading various excuses. Myron kept to himself in his small apartment, building a bicycle he hoped to have ready for spring. It was nearing completion when the first hints of warmer weather returned, and he got in touch with Carl to see if he wanted to meet at the Broken Ship so he could show him the new bike. Carl agreed and they set a date for the following week.

Carl was there early sitting near the front window again. It was open to the street, this being the first day with temperatures crawling well in to the seventies. There was a sizable crowd and it was louder than usual with the kind of good cheer typically produced by the initial retreat from winter. A fresh crew of folks were there for Wednesday Quiz Night. Jeans, t-shirts, and the occasional tweed jacket replaced heavy coats and scarves, and a feeling of levity permeated. Cable Knit behind the bar had switched to short sleeves and she even smiled at Carl. She looked like Barbi Benton, he decided, and was going to tell Myron as much when he arrived.

Myron pulled up in shorts outside the bar, dismounting his bicycle in practiced fashion before it stopped moving. He locked it to a post in plain view of the front window, not wanting to take any chances having invested about five hundred dollars in parts to put it together.

"Is that a Merlin frame?" Carl asked, glancing outside as Myron sat beside him.

"Titanium," Myron confirmed. "You won't believe this, but some tool kid at work gave it to me for covering two of his shifts. I was over at his apartment and noticed it. He didn't have any idea what it was worth."

Carl put a coaster over his beer and walked outside with Myron to inspect the bike more closely. He knelt down at the curb to check the gears.

"So you heard about Bresnick?" Myron said, and Carl looked up inquiringly. "Killed himself three weeks ago. Hung himself in a closet at his place."

Carl stood up and looked at Myron, an incredulous grin across his face. "Fuck you," he said in disbelief.

"I figured you knew. You'd been in touch with him. The cops called me because they were having trouble contacting his family. Me and his ex-girlfriend were the only numbers on his cell."

They sat at the bar sipping their drinks and saying nothing for a while, listening to the initial, easy rounds of the quiz. Lead vocalist and rhythm guitarist for the seminal English punk rock band The Clash. Even under normal circumstances it would have been too obvious to acknowledge.

"You might've been the last one to see the guy alive," Myron said, breaking the silence. "Did he say anything?"

"I don't know," Carl said. "He didn't say much. We hung out at his place and then went for a beer. Feels weird to know that I was inside the same place where he did it."

"So there was nothing .. no indication or anything?"

"What the fuck. I wasn't paying attention for suicidal tendencies. The guy was never much of a talker. He was doing laundry. I think he said something about an Etch A Sketch later at the bar .. you know, the toy? He said it was cool how you could shake the thing and erase the lines."

"Deep," Myron said. "You didn't say anything to him, did you? I mean that might have set him off."

Carl finished his beer and looked up at Myron. A quartet of girls sitting at a table against the wall squealed in delight at having won the first round of the quiz. "Hey you're the prick," he said accusingly. "What the fuck would I ever say to Andy? I think I may have told him how good he had it, if that was so awful. He didn't play to the bullshit anyway, the way guys do." He looked for the bartender to get him another beer, but she was handing out sheets of paper for the second round and flirting with a group of guys.

"Old Andy," Carl said. "Guess he had a bit of Richard Cory in him."

"Old Andy?" Myron said. "Richard Cory? So now you're fucking Morgan Freeman referencing bad poetry?"

They drank later than usual that night, Carl having stepped outside to call Catherine and explain the circumstances. Each subsequent wave of customers seemed to infuse more energy to the place as they sat silently watching. They ordered a final round, beers with a shot, and the bartender smiled and told them it was on the house, cheerfully rapping the bar top with her knuckle.

"Don't you think she looks like Barbi Benton when she smiles?" Carl asked Myron.

"I don't know," he said. "I don't think I've ever seen her smile before. Who's Barbi Benton?"

Myron unchained his bike outside the bar as Carl watched . "Give me a call next week if you want to get together."

"I think I'll walk home tonight. What do you think it is from here .. maybe three miles?"

"Sounds about right," Myron said, and he pedaled off in the opposite direction.

Carl put his hands in his pockets and set off down the street, noting the activity of the subway station below through the sidewalk grill. It was a nice night to be outside.

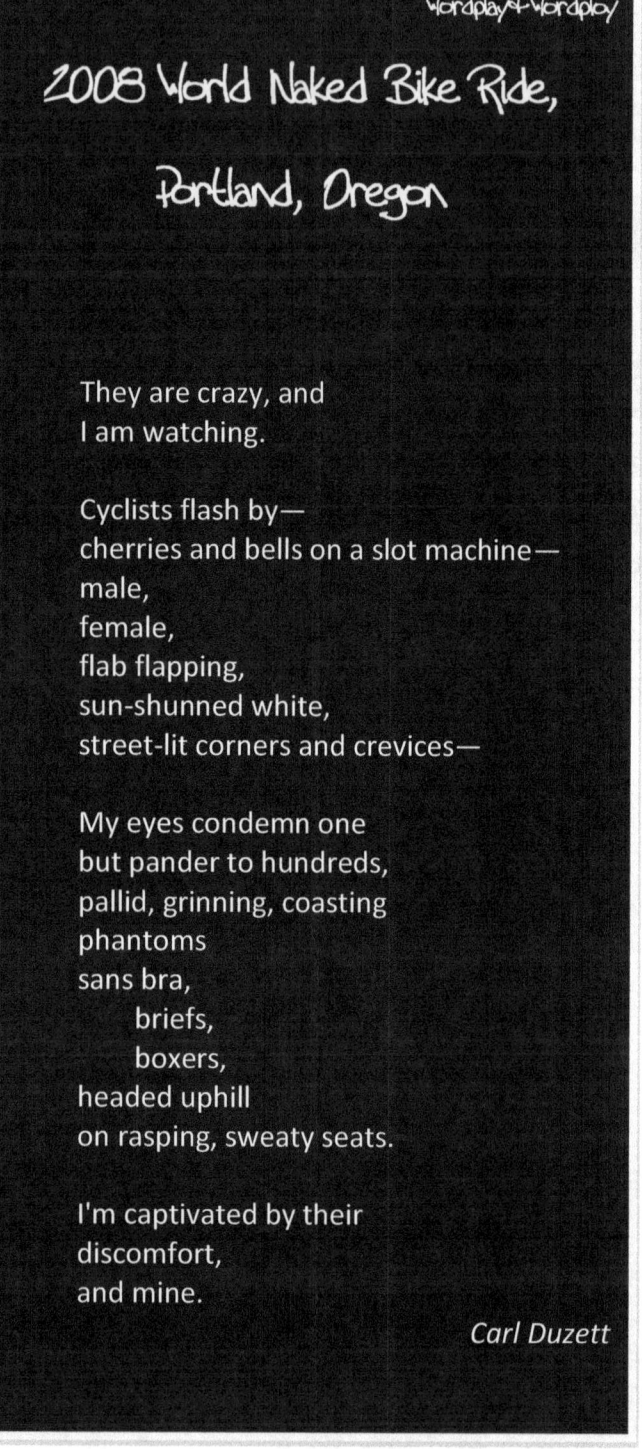

Wordplay+Wordplay

2008 World Naked Bike Ride, Portland, Oregon

They are crazy, and
I am watching.

Cyclists flash by—
cherries and bells on a slot machine—
male,
female,
flab flapping,
sun-shunned white,
street-lit corners and crevices—

My eyes condemn one
but pander to hundreds,
pallid, grinning, coasting
phantoms
sans bra,
    briefs,
    boxers,
headed uphill
on rasping, sweaty seats.

I'm captivated by their
discomfort,
and mine.

Carl Duzett

Blacktop Dreams

Our freshly paved
streets are embedded
with decaying seashells
mixed into thick black tar

Daddy wears ocean rot
and Mamma dreams
of Chanel
but sweat is sweet enough
most days

Oh, shit, she says, *you dunno*
you dunno nothin' she says
to her bloodied fingers,
to her peeling skin

there are fish bones
embedded in the seashells
sinking deeper into the tar
with every footfall
each tire roll

And Daddy's rubber boots
stink up the front porch
speaking only to the flies
you don't know shit,
the rubbery voice whispers
in tones full of sea-deep
death

songs like shell against shell
crumbled to dust underfoot
a tune never swept back
at low tide, never taken wing
like some sky-bound fish

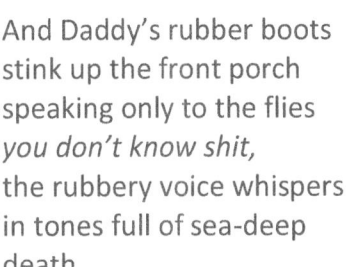

and the flies hum prayers
worried wings sing
loitering hymns
and a buzzing sermon to

the yellow flickering altar
at a bare bulb porch
light

sinking deep into the tar
beneath the naked feet of
girls with lopsided braids
and boys with toothless smiles
swatting at the flies with one hand
while the other turns the
ragged skipping rope.

Mary Mack dressed in black
One, Two, Buckle my shoes…

And Daddy says *oh, hell,*
oh shit, he says,
you dunno nothin' 'bout nothin'
salt grinds between crumbling teeth
like a fistful of sand
sifted from his muddy depths

hopscotch and jump rope
on steaming black asphalt
seashells trapped in tar
fishbones trapped in
seashells

baked into blacktop dreams
until uneven braids
and crooked smiles
melt like warm jelly
into the newly paved road
petrified like so much bone

fishbones and seashells
and the gospels of flies
all saying,
you don't know nothin'
no—they say

you dunno shit.

Harmoni McGlothlin

Notes Magazine's Spotlight Author Suvi Mahonen

About the Spotlight Author

Name: Suvi Mahonen
Age: 38
Location: Queensland, Australia
Hometown: Airlie Beach
Profession/Occupation: Freelance writer

Q&A

Q: You are lost in the dessert, the situation is terminal. The Fates appear and offer you a single word to leave behind, written in the sand but never washed away with the tide; a single word to encompass your life's work-- what would that word be?
A: Help!

Our featured author for this issue, Suvi Mahonen, holds a Master's degree in Writing & Literature from Deakin University in Australia.

Suvi is an international writer with works appearing in a number of literary magazines and online outlets in Australia (including *Island, LiNQ, Verandah*), the UK (*East of the Web*), the U.S. (recently on *MetroMoms*), Canada (*All Rights Reserved*) and Chile (*Southern Pacific Review*).

Suvi has also worked as a journalist in Australia and Canada and has published many feature articles, reviews and travel stories. One of her short stories, 'Bobby', was included in *The Best Australian Stories 2010*.

Featured in this issue of Notes, you will find an interview along with a selection of stories, true and fictional. More of her work can be found on her webpage at:
www.redbubble.com/people/suvimahonen

Q: How long have you been writing?
A: I've been writing since I first learned the alphabet, really. I love stories and was always happiest as a child when I was lost in a book. I think it's a natural progression for many primary school children who enjoy reading to have a go at writing something themselves. Of course the difference back then was that writing was fun. Now it feels like hard work a lot of the time!

Q: Was there a particular moment when you knew this was something you would pursue?
A: Probably when I received my first cheque in the mail for a freelance article I'd placed in an arts and culture magazine in Canada was the moment I thought writing would be something I could pursue. There was a certain kind of validation in being able to earn some income from the words

I'd written, aside from the satisfaction of simply having completed a piece of work.

Q: You write both fiction and nonfiction. Which do you prefer? Why?

A: When I was working as a journalist, I found writing nonfiction articles a lot easier than fiction. You often have a solid framework for a story that revolves around a place or a person you've interviewed, and people give you the most fascinating quotes when you take the time to really listen to them. I also love the research that comes with writing a lot of articles. Despite that, though, I still prefer the challenge of fiction. I think fiction has so much potential to uncover the deepest layers of what makes us human beings, and can take us into the mind and the world of a character in quite a unique way. I've often thought that you generally get more truth in fiction than you do from autobiographies.

Q: Please briefly discuss with us your creative process. What triggers generally act as inspiration for you? How much time do you spend writing on a daily/weekly basis?

A: Every day is different, and I very much have to fit writing in around the demands of life. For example, we've just recently moved from our home in the Dandenong Ranges in Victoria to Airlie Beach in Queensland, and it's taken quite some time to find our feet in a new community. When I was studying for my Master's degree I had to be very disciplined about completing assignments on time. Now that I've finished I sometimes have to push myself to work on a piece of writing, even if I don't feel like it. Reading helps as it can be very inspiring to delve into the mind of a real master. At the moment I'm reading Toni Morrison's amazing novel 'Beloved', and it's the sort of work that keeps resonating in your thoughts long after you've absorbed the words.

Q: Notes is publishing a variety of your works in this issue's Spotlight Feature. Of those, which is your personal favourite? Why?

A: 'Steps to Remembrance' is an article I wrote for a unit in Travel Writing that I undertook as part of my degree at uni, and it's probably my favourite piece of the four Notes is publishing here. I wanted to highlight how tough conditions were for soldiers in the Second World War and how many of our complaints today are trivial compared with what they had to endure. I think we tend to get so caught up in our own lives that we forget the sacrifices made by our troops serving in war-torn countries. I think it's worth taking a moment to remember and to be grateful for what we have.

Q: Several of your short stories revolve around pregnancy/tragedy themes. Could you share with our readers the inspiration and importance of this work to you, personally and artistically?

A: The inspiration to write about pregnancy and the sometimes tragic events that can occur in relation to this comes straight from my husband's work as an obstetrician. He witnesses all kinds of scenarios in the large public hospital where he consults, and some of the stories are deeply touching. Recently my husband has come on board with me on the writing (when he can!) and we've published a couple of collaborative pieces together. It gives us a challenging project to work on as a couple, and is valuable time for us just to be together and to communicate.

Q: Most important question of them all: favourite curse word?

A: Fuck. Definitely fuck. Sometimes that's the only word that sums it up!

One Last Celebration

by Suvi Mahonen

I'm brushing my teeth when I hear the crunch of tyre on gravel. Kyle looks startled when he opens the door.

'Hi honey,' he says. He tries to kiss my cheek.

I lean away. 'You're late.'

'Sorry. Got stuck in an operation.' He locks the door and bends to take off his shoes. 'How's bub?'

'Why didn't you ring?'

'Sorry.' He puts his shoes in the shoe chest. 'I didn't get a chance.'

He starts heading towards the living room. 'Something smells nice,' he says. 'What did you have for dinner?'

I throw the toothbrush at him. It misses and hits the stairs.

'You want to know what I had?' I yell. Fine flecks of toothpaste foam fly from my mouth. 'One little square of cheese. That's all.'

'What are you brushing your teeth for then?'

I let out a scream of frustration. I go over to pick up my toothbrush.

'Hon, what's the matter?' He holds out his hand to help me up. I ignore it. I point the toothbrush at him.

'You can make your own dinner. I'm never going to waste time on you again.' I storm back to the bathroom.

'Honey.' He's right behind me. I slam the door in his face.

I'm all sweaty now. I undress, turn on the shower and get in. I close my eyes and breathe out as the water hits my cheeks.

By the time I've gotten out and into fresh PJs I feel calmer.

I find him at the table eating a bowl of instant noodles. 'I'm sorry I didn't call,' he says with his mouth full.

'Well don't do it again,' I say, pulling out a chair and sitting down.

He chews and swallows. 'What's with the fancy plates and candle?'

'I had this crazy idea that we could have a nice sit-down dinner together,' I say. 'You know, one last celebration where it's just the two of us.'

'I'm really sorry,' he says, staring into his bowl.

'It's not your fault,' I say, rubbing under my ribcage where it's burning. 'I guess you can't help it if you're stuck in an operation.'

He tips his bowl back and drinks the juice.

'Is she okay?' I ask.

'Who?'

'The patient you were stuck with,' I say. 'What was it, a cancer operation?'

'Something like that,' he says. He gets up and goes to the sink.

'Do you want anything else?' I ask.

'No thanks.' He glances at the clock. 'I'm going to have a shower and then go to bed.'

I sit while he washes his dishes. My hands are itchy. I feel queasy. My head is starting to throb.

'Was it ovarian cancer?' I ask.

'Sorry?'

'The case you were stuck with. Was it ovarian cancer?'

He reaches for the tea towel. 'Actually it was a couple of Caesareans,' he says, his back turned to me.

I'm confused. And headachy. And tired. And nauseous. And over it.

'What were you doing on labour ward?' I ask. 'I thought you were still doing your gynaecology oncology rotation.'

'I am,' he says. His face looks flushed. 'One of the consultants asked me to assist her though.'

'That's not fair,' I say. 'Why wasn't someone else rostered on to help her?'

He opens the fridge and takes out a bottle of water. He takes a long swig. I'm standing glaring at him when he closes the door.

'Were they private patients?'

'Why?'

'Why?' I'm yelling again. 'You know why! You promised you wouldn't do any more private assisting.'

'Settle down Bunny.'

I jab him in the chest. 'Don't you "settle down" me! I spent hours in the kitchen making a nice dinner and you let it go to waste.'

'Look, I'm sorry. I wish you'd told me.'

'So it's my fault is it?' I yell. 'It's my fault you'd rather spend time at work than with your family.'

'I never said that,' he pleads. 'Anyway, I didn't look for private assisting okay? She just rung up and asked me.'

I stamp my foot. 'Then why didn't you say no?'

'Look, I'm sorry.' He's sounding impatient now. 'I'm going to have my shower.'

He's halfway up the stairs when he turns back. 'Why do you think I said yes?' he says. 'There's a little thing called money, you know. You use it to buy things like food and electricity and clothes and stuff. If you earned some for once you'd know what it is.'

He keeps heading up. By the time I scream out 'Arsehole' he's disappeared.

I'm sweaty again. My body feels like it's been stuffed in a barrel and thrown over a cliff. I need to lie down.

Upstairs in our bedroom I curl up on top of the doona. I feel so miserable I can't lie still. I get up and go down the hallway to the nursery. As I walk past the bathroom door I kick it.

I sit in the recliner couch. I shut my eyes and count my breathing. A whirring ball of sharp panic is growing in my chest. I scratch and scratch my palms until I force myself to stop. I open my eyes and focus on the stuffed toys. I look at Paddington, I look at his wellington boots, his red hat, the note pinned to his coat. 'Please look after this bear. Thank you.' Please look after … Please … Please … It's not working. I look at the jumperoo instead. That doesn't help either and now I feel like crying. I give my bump a jiggle and wait.

I am crying when Kyle comes in, dressed in his tartan boxers and Bonds T-shirt. He comes over and sits on the recliner's arm rest and runs his fingers through my hair.

'Why do I keep doing it?' he says.

I wipe my nose on my sleeve. 'Doing what?'

'Being a cranky arsehole.'

Despite myself I smile. I reach and take his hand.

He squeezes my fingers. We don't say anything for a while. I look at the empty picture frame waiting for our photo. I start sniffling again.

'Hon.' Kyle kneels down in front of me. 'What is it?'

'I'm scared,' I say.

He rests his hand on my bump. 'Try not to be,' he says softly. 'I won't let anything happen to the two of you.'

'You promise?'

'I promise.'

He leans forward. He kisses the bump. He rests his head against me. 'Only a couple of days to go,' he says.

I smile. I stroke his hair. I run my fingers over where it's thinning.

We stay like this for ages.

Eventually he looks up.

'Bub's having a snooze,' he says.

I frown. 'I know,' I say. 'I've hardly felt any movement all afternoon.'

The lights in the room are dim. Outside the night sky is black. The midwife's half turned away from me. Her shoulder-length brown hair casts a shadow across her face. I lie still holding my breath. As we all stare at the CTG I'm desperate for a sound other than the distortion and the static.

Suddenly there's something else. 'There!' I sit up and point at the machine. 'There!'

'Please lie back down.' The midwife puts pressure on my shoulder. 'Let me check your pulse.' She fumbles for my wrist. Her name's Nikki. She's young, mid-twenties. She shakes her head. 'No, that's your heartbeat.' Her eyes are wide. She looks scared and out of her depth.

The CTG squeals as she squirts more gel on the probe. She tries listening above my bellybutton this time. It still sounds the same— hisses and pops, like white noise from a TV. My throat feels tight. I'm almost at the point of screaming.

I look up at Kyle. He's dressed in the crumpled work clothes that he fished out of the laundry hamper before our quick drive down to Mount Surrey. His forehead's furrowed. 'Let me have a go,' he says. He reaches for the probe. Nikki snatches it away and clutches it to her chest.

'I'm not allowed to,' she says.

He folds his arms and glares at her.

I close my eyes and try counting my breaths. I feel Nikki pressing in with the probe, waiting, angling, waiting, moving on to another spot. Nothing matters except hearing that heartbeat. My own is deafening, the blood surging through my ears.

'Oh for fuck's sake!' Kyle shouts. My eyes fly open. He storms over to the window and slaps his palm against the glass.

Nikki stands up. 'Look,' she says, her hands trembling. 'I understand you're worried but you need to calm down.'

'And you need to know what you're doing!' Kyle yells. 'If you can't work the fucking machine then go get someone who can.'

Nikki looks like she's about to cry. She turns and hurries out of the room.

'Why can't we hear the heartbeat?' I say. My voice breaks. Kyle comes over, turns the CTG machine off then back on, turns the volume up and re-plugs the probe's lead. He's pressing it firmly into my belly when Nikki comes back. She's got another midwife with her.

'My name's Helen. I'm the midwife in charge,' the other midwife says in a firm voice. She's much older. Around sixty. Medium height, solid build, short curly grey hair. Kyle ignores her. She taps him on the shoulder. 'What do you think you're doing?' she says.

He looks up briefly, lips thin. She reaches for the probe. He pushes her hand away.

'Don't,' he says. 'I know what I'm doing.'

'I'm not debating that,' she says. 'But you know you're not allowed to treat family.'

'Ssh!' He holds his finger to his lips. He keeps searching.

Helen reaches over and switches the machine off. Kyle turns, his face livid.

'I'll call security,' Nikki says, poised near the door.

'Don't be stupid,' Helen snaps. She turns back to Kyle and speaks gently. 'You need to pull yourself together. You're upsetting your wife.'

He looks at me, eyes wild, he looks at her, he looks back at me. 'Where's Dr. Auburn?'

'He's coming,' Helen says. She touches his shoulder. 'Now come on, take a seat. I'll have a listen but you need to try and stay calm.'

Kyle nods. Eyes on the ground. I'm so scared I feel like retching.

'Now first things first sweety,' Helen says. 'Sit up for a sec.' As I lean forward she plumps the pillows behind me and asks Nikki to go check on room seven.

When it's just the three of us she switches on the machine. The screen flickers then glows a faint blue.

She squirts gel on the probe. She looks up and tries to smile.

'Now let's see what we can hear.'

'I need some water,' I murmur.

I'm slumped over the beanbag. Kyle's rubbing my neck. 'Here hon.' He brings the straw to my lips.

I can feel another contraction coming. A tight excruciating cramp. It starts in my belly and spreads all over. I close my eyes and rock back and forth on my knees. I bury my face in the beanbag and groan. I take in a deep breath and push.

'That's the way,' Helen says behind me.

My arms are shaking. I gasp and push again.

The contraction is starting to ease. I pant, open my eyes. Focus on Kyle's jeans.

A heavier hand rests on my back. Dr Auburn's bent down face comes into view. 'That last push was very good Sara,' he says. 'We're starting to see some hair.' I nod. I'm out of breath.

Dr Auburn steps away. Kyle strokes my cheek. 'I'm really proud of you honey.' I reach up and squeeze his hand. He squeezes back gently, avoiding the needle in the back of mine.

I let go when I feel another contraction building. I bite the beanbag. It tastes like vinyl and soap.

'That's it.' Helen's voice. 'Let your body tell you what to do.'

I bear down. I strain so hard I see red. It's burning. It's stinging. I take a shuddering breath. The urge is still there. I push again. More pain.

After it's gone I lie there sobbing. Kyle wipes my forehead. 'It's okay hon,' he says. 'You're almost there.'

'Do you want to try another position sweety?' Helen asks.

I shake my head. All of a sudden nausea hits me. I lean forward and vomit.

'I'm sorry.' I start crying again. Drool runs from my nose.

'Don't be silly,' she says. 'I'll just get you to sit up.'

Kyle helps me to turn around so I'm sitting upright on the birthmat. He supports my back while I hang my head between my knees. I hear Helen wiping up behind me.

Another contraction is coming. I start to panic.

'Don't waste your energy,' Dr Auburn says. 'Push!'

My body takes over. Pain and pressure roll forward. My teeth clenched. Eyes shut. Chin on my chest. Every muscle fibre straining. There's so much pressure now. I feel myself give way.

Helen's kneeling between my legs. She looks up at me.

'That's it sweety,' she says. 'The head's nearly out.'

Later that morning there's a soft knock on the door.

I'm sitting in the armchair. Kyle's on a chair facing me. Benny's in the cot between us. We've been like this for the past hour. Not talking. Just looking. Not knowing what to say.

Kyle goes and opens the door. It's Dr Auburn. He's in a fresh white shirt and clean pants.

'How are you feeling?' he asks.

I don't say anything.

'I'm sorry.' He stands there, fingers fidgeting, like he's not sure what to say next.

'I need to ask you two a difficult question,' he finally says.

'Is it about an autopsy?' Kyle says.

'Yes.'

Kyle's hand tightens on my shoulder. I sit there. Nothing seems real.

'Have you examined him?' Kyle asks.

'I did earlier,' Dr Auburn says.

'And ...?'

'There's nothing obvious. Though it's hard to tell when...' He stops and studies his thumbs.

'When do we have to decide by?' Kyle says.

Dr Auburn glances at Benny. 'No rush,' he says. 'Tomorrow morning will be fine.'

I look out the window at the grey sky.

'I don't want to stay another night.' My voice is hoarse.

'You don't have to,' Dr Auburn says. He sounds apologetic. 'But I'd prefer if you did.'

'Why?'

'I'd like to see some improvement in your liver and renal function profile first.'

I close my eyes and lean my head back.

'Plus it will give you a chance to see the social worker,' I hear him say.

'What for?'

'To help you with the forms and funeral arrangements. And also to provide you with options for counselling.'

'I'm already seeing a psychologist,' I say, my eyes still closed.

'Okay.' There's a pause. His shoes squeak. 'Is there anything you wanted to ask me?'

I count my breaths.

'Sara?'

I shake my head.

'Once again I'm terribly sorry for what's happened.' His voice rises. 'I'll see you later then.'

'Thanks,' Kyle says. I feel him lean forward. I imagine them shaking hands.

'Good bye Sara,' Dr Auburn says. His footsteps head towards the door.

'Why didn't you induce me?'

'Honey.' Kyle squeezes my shoulder. I ignore him.

Dr Auburn stands still, face straight, with his hand on the doorknob. He comes back over and sits down on the edge of the bed.

'I can understand your anger,' he says.

'I'm not angry,' I say. 'I just want to know why.'

'When I saw you last Wednesday,' he says cautiously, 'there wasn't really an indication.'

'What do you mean there wasn't an indication?' I yell. Dr Auburn recoils. 'What about being alive? He was still alive!'

I drop my face in my hands and cry. And cry. Kyle strokes my hair but I barely notice.

Eventually I slow down. I take a handful of tissues and blow my nose.

'Now look.' Dr Auburn leans forward and touches my knee. 'I'll come back and talk to you later this evening, okay?'

I nod.

He stands up again. 'Now try and get some rest.'

After he leaves Kyle squats down in front of me.

'How about I pop out for a couple of hours,' he says. 'Give you a chance to nap.'

I look at our son lying there. His little face peeking out between his red pom-pom cap and his blanket.

'I want to hold him again,' I say.

'Honey.' Kyle squeezes my hand. He looks into my eyes. 'How about later. Have a rest first.'

'No,' I say. 'I can rest for the rest of my life. But I've only got Benny for today.'

Spreading Our Wings

by Suvi Mahonen

It was a bright and clear February morning. A soft southerly breeze was blowing in from over the lake, forming wavelets that lapped against the sandy shore. The air smelt faintly of sea salt and mud, and the leaves of the stunted gums that grew between the water's edge and the back garden were trembling.

I was out on the veranda enjoying the sun when I first heard it. Shading my eyes I watched as the World War II Tiger Moth came into view, its double-decker wings cutting a line across the sky. From where I was the putter of its engine sounded less like an aircraft and more like a lawnmower in need of an oil change. It was nearly out of sight when suddenly the engine pitch changed and the plane went into a nosedive. I held my breath as it hurtled towards the ground. Just when it seemed it would be too late the plane levelled out, swung steeply up, and then over in a 360 degree upside-down loop.

I glanced over to where Annie was standing on the top step.

'I can't believe he paid extra for that,' I said.

She looked at me with her bright brown eyes but didn't say anything. No stranger to flying herself, she didn't seem perturbed.

When my husband returned, flush with excitement, he showed me a photo. There he was, standing in a field in front of the Tiger Moth, dressed Red Baron style in a pair of goggles and a leather jacket and cap.

I wondered if the pilot made much money from taking tourists on joyrides.

'I'm not sure,' my husband said. 'I think he mainly does it because he loves flying. He also works as a mechanic.'

Travelling around Australia I've noticed that small country towns seem to attract people who wear many hats. And I don't mean literal hats—your Akubra, your hard hat, your beanie—either. I mean people who have the desire, or versatility, or both, to work in more than one job.

Take Janet for example. Janet was a sheep farmer, wife and mother of five. She was also the owner, cleaner and manager of 'Lake's Edge,' our holiday accommodation in Robe.

Robe is a small harbour town located on the South Australian Limestone Coast approximately 325 km south east of Adelaide. Since we live in a high bushfire risk area in Victoria, we'd decided to spend our two week's summer holiday somewhere where we wouldn't have to be regularly checking CFA updates and activating our bushfire survival plan. With a population of approximately 2000 spread along white sandy beaches and between lakes and rocky coves, and with its open surrounding expanses of grazing land and vineyards, Robe seemed a perfect place.

'Come in, come in,' Janet had said, beckoning from the doorway as we got out of our car. 'I'll show you around.' A vivacious, petite, forty-something blonde, she was wearing a black dress and strappy heels, even though she told us she'd just finished vacuuming.

The three-bedroom beach house style white weatherboard was decorated in a nautical theme. A life buoy hung on one wall, a fishing net on another. Its spacious and open-plan central living area, furnished simply yet comfortably, spoke of lazy afternoons and the opportunity to relax. The sun dipping westward shone through the wide windows, gleaming off the polished floorboards and giving the whole place a warm glow.

We went out onto the back veranda where Janet showed off the view. A garden path sloped down across manicured lawn, past rose bushes and clusters of nasturtiums and into a patch of tea trees and gums. Just beyond lay the waters of Lake Fellmongery.

'Look!' I said excitedly.

'What?'

'Doesn't matter,' I said, embarrassed. The magpie had flown away.

Janet told us that she and her husband had built 'Lake's Edge' five years ago and they were planning to eventually retire here. As she chatted about the house and herself, I wondered how she'd ever find the time to retire. Her exuberant energy spread to so many hats. Along with the sheep farming and child raising, she also worked as a marriage and civil celebrant and made and sold her own wine. On top of all that she was an artist as well. Her sketches, collages and paintings—each with a little price tag—brightened the walls of every room in the house.

'This one's really cute,' I said, pointing to a small oil of a frog doing a handstand.

Janet beamed.

When her tour was done she told us to relax and enjoy ourselves. Then she headed off in a whirl of blonde hair and black hem to go kayaking.

Later that afternoon I spotted the magpie again. I was a fan of these noisy Australian larrikins and had 'adopted' a pair who roosted in tall gums beyond the back of our property at home. Twice a day they'd land on the back door mat and sing until I let them in and hand fed them pieces of cheese. We'd named them Heckle and Jeckle. And I was missing them already. In compensation I set out to befriend the local magpie family in-between our outings.

One of the games my husband and I played was walking into the town centre and pretending we'd travelled back to the 19th century. It wasn't as hard as you'd think. Robe was founded in 1846 and many of its old buildings are still standing. These include the 'Our Lady of the Sea Chapel,' built in 1858 and considered to be one of the oldest Catholic churches in South Australia, and the Customs House, built in the 1860s when Robe was the second busiest port in South Australia.

We'd start off from the village green and wander down Smillie Street, the historical main road, past limestone shops with their Victorian facades and cottages with their bursting English gardens. Given it was still the tail end of summer we were pleasantly surprised by the subdued quietness of the streets. We'd end up on the lawns of the Royal Circus next to the town's harbour and nibble on cheese and dark chocolate that we'd picked up at one of the delicatessens along the way. If it was a hot afternoon we'd then pop into the Caledonian Inn for a cold drink. A grand two-storey stone building, it was built in 1859 partly from wood salvaged from local shipwrecks.

These used to be a frequent occurrence in the surrounding Guichen Bay. To serve as a warning landmark for passing ships a limestone structure named the Obelisk was built in 1855. One overcast morning we drove out to nearby Cape Dombey to see it. The Obelisk was both an odd and impressive sight. Over ten metres tall and shaped like a pyramid, it was painted in giant red and white stripes. Picking our way across the narrow crated peninsula we walked up as close as we could.

When we got there I stood, arms folded, against the stiff southerly breeze. White caps stretched out into the grey horizon and gulls circled in the sky, their screeches merging with the roar of the waves smashing against the cliffs. The limestone walls were decaying, their bases slanting inwards from the corrosive effect of the sea. And the ledge on which the Obelisk sat was noticeably tilting.

I shivered and took a step back.

During our stay in Robe we returned to the Obelisk a number of times to take evening walks along the trails leading off from the car park. Our favourite headed south along the coastline. Veering inland after a blowhole, it would then head back up through dense growths of coastal wattle and daisy bush before ending at the ruins of the Old Gaol.

One time we took a breather, sitting in the sand with our backs against a wind-smoothed rock and our legs stretched out facing the sea. The air was warm and stirring softly, carrying with it the scent of nearby flowering heath. Lines of thin white cloud lay across the deepening sky and the sun hung low, casting beams of crimson orange over the water. In the cove beneath us the retreating tide frothed and sloshed gently against the rock pools. Amongst the swells, a small dark shape bobbed in the distance. A red light shone from its bow.

'I wonder what kind of boat that is?' I said.

My husband squinted. 'It could be a lobster trawler,' he said.

We lapsed back into silence.

'I'm hungry,' he said several minutes later.

There were plenty of choices when it came to dining in Robe. Some nights we'd fire up the barbecue and cook juicy steaks from the local butcher. Other nights we'd eat at one of the eleven different restaurants in town. Once we even lashed out and had fresh lobster at The Sails. To call it fresh was an understatement. With a lobster fleet based in Robe, what you ate in the evening had usually been caught that morning.

Whenever we invited Barry and Sally and their daughter Annie to eat at 'Lake's Edge' the food we served was nowhere near as fancy.

Bread crusts and squares of cheese. Our guests still seemed to love it though.

They were the local magpie family that I'd managed to bribe into friendship. By our second week in Robe we'd reached a point in our relationship where they'd come onto the back steps to eat as long as I promised not to move. They wouldn't come onto the veranda though or take food from my hand.

'Don't take it personally,' my husband said. 'They're a lot smaller here. Maybe they're not as bold.'

He was right. South Australian magpies were smaller than Victorian ones. I wondered how a magpie ended up on the South Australian state flag.

'We could go to the library and google it,' my husband said.

I didn't want to. It was satisfyingly retro to ignore the internet and our email accounts for a whole two weeks. And it was pleasing to read words off a page instead of a computer screen for a change. We spent plenty of time with our books out on the veranda or under a tree at the beach. In between these bursts of exertion we'd swim in the ocean, indulge in massages and browse the local antique shops and art galleries. It wasn't all hard work though. We also went on day trips to sample the wares of the Coonawarra wineries and look at the megafauna fossils in the world heritage listed Naracoorte Caves.

Janet dropped by one afternoon towards the end of our stay to give us some fresh lamb chops from their farm. I told her about Barry, Sally and Annie. She was delighted. She already provided containers of seed and pellets at 'Lake's Edge' so guests could feed the lorikeets and ducks. Now the magpies could join the list.

By now they were coming onto the veranda to eat, but they still weren't taking food from my hand. One more week and I think I would have had them.

But I was missing our own.

The first thing I did when we got back home was to go into the backyard and refill the birdbath that the magpies liked to drink out of. I stood and waited but couldn't see or hear them anywhere.

Disappointed, I went inside.

'What if they've gone?' I said.

'They won't have,' my husband said. 'Remember once magpies have established their territory they never leave.'

I was glad we were different than that. Imagine never getting out and exploring the rest of Australia. Never meeting interesting people like Janet. Never spending time in a place like Robe.

It wasn't until just before sunset, when we were unpacking our suitcases, that we heard them.

'C'mon,' I said, grabbing my husband's arm.

We went downstairs.

There they were, Heckle and Jeckle, singing at our back door.

Two months later, when the rains had returned, the lawn was reviving and the leaves were starting to curl, I received a parcel in the post.

'What is it?' my husband asked.

'No idea,' I said, ripping open the brown wrapping paper.

Inside was the oil painting of the frog doing a handstand along with a small card. On it Janet had simply written:

Enjoy.

Blocks of Couverture

by Suvi Mahonen

Mid-morning sun angles in through the office window, casting a warm line across the surface of Dr Barker's desk. It catches the back of his head and shoulders, making the tips of his curly grey hair glow. He's hunched forward, holding the phone receiver to his ear. In his other hand an uncapped pen bounces between two fingers.

He sighs. 'Still holding,' he says, covering the mouthpiece with his hand. His elbow bumps one of the several loose clusters of papers and manila folders on his desk. His computer's switched off. Post-it notes are stuck to the monitor. They blur.

I blink. My eyes feel like fibreglass. I try to focus by looking around the room. Blue carpet. Cream coloured walls. The examination couch on my left. Behind us, near the door, a large bookshelf crammed with textbooks and journals. In the corner a sink, a metal bin.

'Yes. This is Dr Geoff Barker.'

I turn back.

'I'm after a first trimester screening result.' He leans back in his leather chair. There's a pause. 'Dani Jackson.' He gives them my date of birth and address. There's a much longer pause.

I look at Mark for reassurance. His lips are thin. His jaw's clenched at a boxy angle and the collar of his red polo top is bent.

Dr Barker jots down some numbers on a pad of paper. 'Thank you.' He hangs up. 'Sorry about that.'

I attempt a smile.

He leans forward and clasps his hands and looks at me. 'Unfortunately your baby's nuchal fold translucency was a little thicker than average,' he says.

My left hand starts to tremble. I steady it with my right. I sit, looking at Dr Barker, feeling them twitch in my lap.

'Do you understand what I mean by that?'

'It ...' I clear my throat. 'It means the skin at the back of the baby's neck is too thick.'

'That's correct.' He glances at the numbers on the pad of paper. 'Often it can occur in babies that turn out to be perfectly healthy and normal. But there is also a known association with foetal chromosomal anomalies.'

'So what's the risk?' Mark asks.

Dr Barker hesitates. He glances at Mark but addresses me.

'As you may remember me explaining to you at your first antenatal visit, the results of the nuchal fold thickness are combined with the placental hormone levels blood test that you had done last week.'

I nod. My tongue's so dry it feels swollen.

'This enables an odds ratio to be calculated of the chances of your baby having Trisomy 21, more commonly known as Down syndrome, or Trisomy 13 or 18.'

He looks back down at the pad. I try and read the numbers but it's too messy a scrawl.

'The risk of your baby having Trisomy 13 came back as one in 2400 and Trisomy 18 as one in 1150. That's slightly higher than average for your age but still very low.'

I don't want to hear what's right. I need to know what's wrong. 'What about Down syndrome?' I say.

He blinks. 'One in forty.' The shoulder line of his thin striped blue suit sags slightly, as if somehow it's his fault.

The trembling in my lap gets stronger. Mark reaches over and covers my hands with his own.

I sit here as the sun line creeps closer towards me, feeling a weird combination of relief and fear.

One in forty.

It could have been worse. It could have been worse.

It's still pretty bad.

'So what now?' I say.

Every action has its consequences. Every journey has its end.

I don't really remember much about our drive back home. I think I cried a bit. But mostly I just sat there feeling numb.

My fantasy world had collapsed.

This morning I was Dani Jackson. Thirty-six. In good health and have-to-work-at-it-but-still-reasonable shape. Contentedly married to Mark, my dependable, handsome, hardworking husband. We lived in a large, quirky, stone and timber house in the midst of a mountainous forest. And I loved my job, running a small but expanding artisan chocolate-making business. But, most important of all, after years of pain and chaos and memories forgotten, and then, after all that, a year of trying and waiting and almost giving up, I was finally pregnant and we were going to become a family.

I told you it was a fantasy world.

So here I am. Tuesday. Eight pm. About to have a shower. Standing in the bathroom, staring in the mirror at Dani Jackson. Thirty-six. Plain, bordering on ugly. Creases deepening, cellulite spreading, crooked nose and blotchy skin. In a difficult-at-times eight-years-and-counting marriage to Mark Jackson, a thirty-eight year old short-tempered workaholic who's still studying and training because of unresolved issues and a tendency towards indecision. The house we live in is cold and dark and expensive to run. And as for my business, no one takes it seriously and I barely break even, and my dreams of becoming an in-demand maker of award-winning chocolates will almost certainly remain just a dream.

I look away from the pallid woman in the mirror who's standing there dressed only in her underwear. Turning on the tap I splash water on my face and neck. A trickle runs down my cleavage, around my belly button, and stops at the bulge above the elastic of my briefs.

I look down. I rub my hand over my skin.

At least one dream came true.

I can still see it clearly. Our baby's tiny hands. The little lines of light for fingers. Its legs kicking. Its heart beating. The outline of its face.

Why did we wait so long?

The woman in the mirror who won't meet my eye knows of many reasons, some mentionable, some not. Me and Mark got together when I was twenty-five. Got married when I was twenty-eight. And having kids straight away wasn't on either of our horizons. But when I turned thirty I started thinking. And the thinkings became maybes, and the maybes became we should. So I told Mark – and he said no, let's wait a little longer.

And so we waited.

Travel – let's wait a little longer. Career – let's wait a little longer. House deposit – let's wait a little longer. Until Mark's 'a little longers' turned into one big lot longer. And then I forced the issue. And then the not happened.

I peel off my underwear, turn on the shower taps and get in, feeling the pinpricks of hot water on my face. I think about how easy it is to ignore time. How easy it is to be in self-denial. How easy to fool yourself into believing that there's plenty of it left. Until that one day when you finally wake up to yourself, and you're thirty-five, and you realise that your life to this point really hasn't added up to all that much.

And then you start to panic.

Perhaps there was a part of me that didn't mind. In a way I'd enjoyed the solace of mundane thirty-something couple-with-no-children predictability and comfort. Especially after that night at the train station, when for a long time I drew in, drew back, avoiding any confrontation.

Even with my husband.

Eventually though I had to move on. I set things in motion. Flicked a rail switch so to speak. And now our lives were hurtling towards an unknown destination.

Unfortunately we were on separate tracks.

I enter my office and creak the door shut behind me. In the dark I make my way to the desk by feel and boot up the computer and wait for the electronic wheezes and grunts to settle down. By the time I've finished googling chorionic villus sampling, amniocentesis, chromosome analysis and Down syndrome, my headache's worse, my shoulder's burning and the little clock on the bottom right hand corner of the screen says 2:13 a.m.

I stay as I'm sitting, too tired to move, listening to the faint high-pitched hum of the monitor. Eventually the screen saver starts and the room darkens in the fraction of black as it does. Straightening up I grip the mouse and google again.

I find a website called YourPregnancyDotCom. 'We cover everything' the homepage boasts above a photo of a cute dimply baby. I go to the forum section. Registering under 'Confused36' I click on the new topic button and type in 'Unhelpful Husband'. Underneath, in the dialogue box, I type:

My husband's trying to bully me into having a CVS. What do I do?

I press Send.

I sit staring at the screen. It starts going hazy. I scrunch my eyes, rub them, roll them, open them widely. I look at the mug of tea I'd drunk the morning of the ultrasound, the four-day-old tea tag stiff and crusted to its side. I go to shut down. I've poised the arrow over the X when, suddenly:

Re: Unhelpful Husband

pops up on the screen.

I lean forward and squint. Who else would be up and on this website at this time of night? Someone tagged 'PixieBump' apparently. She hasn't minced words:

Leave him :)

Despite myself I smile. I type back:

I was being serious.

A few seconds later:

So was I!

I'm wondering how to respond when another message from PixieBump appears:

Sounds like you're having a shitty time.

I type back:

Yes I am. Very shitty.

PixieBump:

Want to tell?

My fingers race over the keyboard:

We've been trying since the beginning of last year and it's been a long, long slog of ovulation calendars, healthy living, disappointing one-lined pregnancy tests and so many timed sperm deposits that I think even my husband was starting to lose interest. I had almost resigned myself to going down the IVF road when I finally found out I was pregnant. Got some bad news yesterday though – my first

45

trimester test has come back as high risk for Down syndrome and my husband's pressuring me to have a CVS.

I press Send. Several minutes pass. I look at my Koko Black wall calendar. I get up and flip it over to February. When I get back she's replied:

Congratulations on being pregnant!! Sorry your husband's being an arsehole though. Ignore him. It's your choice not his. Men can't understand. They don't have the same bond with pregnancy that we do. Is this your first baby? How many weeks pregnant are you?

For a moment I'm tempted to crawl under the desk and unplug the computer. Instead I count backwards from thirty then type:

Twelve weeks and five days. That's part of the problem. Mark wants me to have a CVS ASAP so we can have time to "think about our options" before I start to show.

PixieBump:

Men can be so tactful. Sounds like he knows what he wants. But what about you?

I pause. Then type:

I don't know. To be honest I'm not sure if Mark definitely knows either. Unfortunately he's the sort of guy who can't tolerate uncertainty and it hurts me that he wants me to have a procedure that's a risk to our baby just so he can find out.

Her response:

It's hard when you're being pressured. BTW I know someone who had a CVS. It's kind of like an amnio isn't it?

My reply:

Yes. But the CVS can be done earlier (10 weeks instead of 15) and it carries twice the risk of causing a miscarriage. Probably because when the needle is stuck in, instead of sampling fluid from around the baby it actually takes a biopsy of the placenta.

It suddenly strikes me that I have no idea who I'm chatting to. I add another line before pressing Send.

What about yourself? How many weeks are you? Do you have any kids?

PixieBump messages back:

Just the one – Andrew. He's three. Plus current bump of course (24 weeks). Judging by the jumping it feels like she'll take after her hyperactive older brother. Speaking of which I'd better go and check on him. The playroom's gone quiet which usually = trouble.

Playroom? I type:

Andrew must be hyperactive if he's up and playing this early in the morning!

The minutes tick by. I sit with only the whine of a mosquito at the window for company. Great. I've just met an online stranger who sounds friendly and now I've gone and insulted her by implying that her son should be on Ritalin. My momentary lift from the unexpected webchat is ebbing away when her reply flashes onto the screen:

> Early in the morning! LOL. It's 3:45 in the afternoon sweety. Where in the world (literally) are you? Found out why the playroom was so quiet – miracle of miracles the little man was asleep!

I choose my words more carefully this time:

> Glad to hear he's napping. I live on the outskirts of Melbourne, Australia. What about you?

PixieBump replies:

> St Albans, aka outer northern outskirts of London, England. Sounds like you should go and have a lie down. I can only imagine what horrible time of night it is down there.

I've been dismissed. With good intentions to be fair but dismissed nonetheless. I can't blame her. She must have better things to do. I'm wondering how to say goodbye in a casual yet grateful kind of way when she posts me a final message:

> BTW my email address is pwoodruff@yahoo.co.uk in case you ever want to chat or debrief about anything. It was great to meet you Confused36. Best of luck. And remember, the choice is up to you.

Two days later I pull into the car park overlooking the dam. Apart from a white ute sitting sideways near the entrance no one else is here. I drive past a set of splintery picnic benches and park at the end behind a green metallic pump shed. Faded yellow lines, crumpled beer cans on the verge, grass growing through bitumen cracks. Below, a crescent of still waters. Beyond, a ragged horizon of trees, a distant plume of smoke.

When I got into the car this morning I just sat there for ages. Windows wound down a few centimetres, keys in the ignition, garage door closed. Eventually I let go of the keys and got out and opened the garage door and got back in and reversed out the driveway. As I shifted into first I was shaking so much I found it hard to steer.

I sit here, engine off and ticking, gripping the gearstick and wheel. My hands start to cramp. I detach them, claw-like, and stretch out my fingers. I look at my indented palms. Trace the lifelines with my eyes.

I think of Darryl, Nicky's older 'little' brother, and how fascinated he was with other people's hands. How he'd try and 'trick' you by saying 'Hi Five'. How he'd grab your hands and measure his stubby fingers against yours. How he always wanted to play thumb wrestle. How he was sometimes too rough.

I remember back to that summer between grades four and five when me and Nicky were best friends. The times we'd push her bed across the door to stop Darryl from coming in. The way we'd keep quiet until the knocks and mushy-mouthed 'Nuckee's' finally went away. Later we'd sneak out to make ourselves Milos. Sometimes a Barbie was missing when we came back. She'd track him down. I'd follow. He'd always be in his same hiding spot, behind the stack of old pallets next to the packing shed. When he'd see us he'd grin and point at Barbie's chest and say 'Boobies', twist open the plastic legs and say 'Bum'. How loud he'd laugh, rivulets of snot. The dull-lidded hurt look on his face when she'd snatch Barbie back and hiss 'Retard'

I sift through other memories, some vivid, some hazy.

The faces our classmates would pull and the noises they'd make whenever the special bus drove past. Nicky crying after being teased that their mum had had sex with an ape. The many times she wasn't at school because Darryl was in Cairns Base with his heart and kidney problems. That Sunday we were all out in Nicky's front yard and the tough boys from high school cycled past and yelled 'Mongo' at Darryl and flicked cigarette butts at him. Darryl laughing, loving the game. The tough boys laughing when they hit his face. The solemn promise I made when Nicky told me that the real reason Toby, their pet dog, had been moved to a farm was because Darryl kept pulling down his pants and letting Toby lick his bum.

I stare out at the glinting blue waters, watch the shadow of a cloud as it slowly passes over. The back of my throat tastes like how rancid coleslaw smells. I power all the windows all the way down. Lean out. Spit.

'At first you don't realise how lucky you really are,' a blogger on a Down syndrome support group forum had said. 'You can't imagine how much joy and love they'll bring to your life. We thank God for trusting us with His wonderful gift.'

I close my eyes and lean back against the headrest.

If there is a god and Down syndrome is so wonderful then how come we're not all born with it?

One in forty.

How convenient. How simple. The chance of your life altering forever. The chance of your life getting so much worse. All boiled down to a simple fraction.

Last night, after Mark went to bed, I took the ultrasound photo – the one Kate seemed so reluctant to print out – off the fridge and went into my office. I kept holding the photo up to the monitor, comparing it to internet pictures of first trimester foetuses with Down syndrome. I don't remember falling asleep, but I do remember dreaming. When I woke up my face was in the keyboard, my legs were totally pins and needley and the computer screen had frozen. I couldn't find the photo. I didn't look for long.

The sun's in my face now. Blood red vision through closed lids. I shade my shut eyes and listen to the corpulent hum of a blowfly. Smell the resin and dry grass.

I wake with a fright, back twinging as I bolt upright, doona spilling off me. As I sit, neck quivering, T-shirt stuck to my skin, the room slowly forms in the fragments of moonlight coming through the trees. Chest of drawers, bookcase, cherry-wood chair in the corner. Mark's sleeping hump next to me.

I pinch the skin at the base of my throat. Squeeze hard until pain flares in my eyes. When my heart finally slows down I check the clock.

It's three fifty-three.

I know what I need to do.

I've already emptied the dishwasher, checked there's enough supplies and swept and mopped the kitchen floor when the alarm goes off. A few minutes later there's footsteps on stairs and Mark appears, lopsided hair and scrumpled boxer shorts.

I'm lining trays with waxed paper.

'Morning.'

'Morning.'

I see him raise an eyebrow at the bottle of corn syrup and the three blocks of dark couverture on the counter. I wait for it.

'I better go have my shower,' he says.

I'm having mine when he leaves for work.

The morning sun is sprawling into the kitchen, burnishing the copper pots and gleaming off the aluminium trays, by the time I start tempering. It's dusk outside and the trays are almost full when Mark comes home.

Already? I glance at the clock. I'm in the middle of dipping truffles. I dunk one into the melted chocolate. Hold it under till it drowns.

'Hi.'

'Hi.'

I look up as he appears around the corner. His dark hair's flattened, the top button of his Baubridge & Kay shirt undone, tie missing in action, smile a little forced.

'Someone's been busy,' he says, looking around the kitchen.

Almost every square inch of the benches and island top are covered with tray after tray of chocolates. There's shiny half globes of pralines, miniature gourmet cups, neat lines of logs in a variety of flavours, crispy clusters of brittle, decorated hand-dipped squares, and a plague of chocolate mice both brown and white. There's also the inevitable mess – a sink overflowing with moulds, spatulas, mixing blades and whisks and a pile of dirty bowls balancing precariously next to it.

'Should we get take out tonight?'

'It's Wednesday,' I say, picking up a sticky ball of ganache and pressing it onto the dipping fork with a little more force than necessary. 'We don't eat take out on Wednesdays.'

He stands there watching me while I dip the ganache into the bowl of melted chocolate and take it out and let it drip. I drop the truffle into the topping pan and roll it back and forth in the cocoa. He keeps watching. I keep rolling.

'What!' I glare at him.

The lines under his eyes are deep, the room behind him dim.

'We need to talk about Friday.'

The cocoa powdering my hands starts to muddy.

'Can't you see I'm busy?'

Another one of his pauses. He glances sideways, exhales slowly through his nose.

'So you've made up your mind then.'

I pick up the tray of lemon mint squares, open the cupboard door beneath the island and slot the tray into the drying rack. I stay squatting for a second, admiring the neatly lined squares of chocolate, the thin slivers of sugared peel set diagonally across each one.

'It's a one in forty chance for goodness sakes,' he says behind me. 'Don't I get a say in this too?'

My knees pop as I stand. I look my husband in the eyes. 'You've already had your say.'

They harden. 'We haven't talked properly and you know it.'

I stare at him. He stares back. He turns and gestures to the couch. 'Can we at least sit down?'

I hesitate.

'Please?'

We go over to the TV nook and sit. Two vague reflected humps on the blank plasma screen. Despite myself I start giggling.

'What's so funny?'

I stop. I bring my feet up and twist around to face him cross-legged. 'You brought me here. You speak.'

'Okay then.' His features smooth out in the light from the kitchen. 'If the baby has Down syndrome I think we should try again.'

'Which means ... '

He flushes. 'You know what it means.'

My eyes start pulsing. 'Say it then!' I yell. I slap his thigh so hard it hurts my hand. 'Say it you coward.'

He recoils. I go to leave. He catches the back of my smock. I claw at his fingers.

'Abortion.'

I stop twisting his thumb.

'There,' he says. 'I've said it. Now sit back down.'

'Not until you let go of me.'

He does. I balance my bum on the armrest and look down at him. He's sitting in my shade, shoulders slumped, head tilted down a fraction.

'If the baby has Down syndrome, then yes, I would prefer if you had a termination.'

'Abortion.'

'Abortion. But I wouldn't pressure you into having one.'

'I don't believe you.'

He looks up at me, eyes surprisingly white. 'Have you really thought about it Dan? Have you thought about how hard it would be? I mean do you really think you could handle it?'

I hop off the couch. Fists clenched.

'Of course I know it would be fucking hard. That doesn't change the fact that it's still our baby.' I point at my belly. 'It's already in there Mark. Don't you feel anything for it for arse sakes? It's as much a part of you as it is of me!'

He leans forward and smothers his face in his hands. 'I know.' Voice muffled. 'It's just …' He looks up, bleary eyed. 'A child with Down syndrome. I'm not sure if I could do it.'

I feel numb. This isn't my husband.

'Yes you can,' I say. 'If you have to you will.'

I stare at him defiantly. Out of my shade he's different. It's night now, and the glow from the kitchen lights illuminates the right side of his face Phantom of the Opera-like. The left side of his face is in darkness.

'I think I know why you won't have the CVS,' he says softly. 'It's not the small risk of miscarrying that's stopping you. I think you'd prefer not to know because if you did find out that the baby has Down syndrome, you'd want to terminate as well.'

It's easier to get angry again than try and deny it. I go to the TV cabinet, pick up a DVD and frisbee it at him.

It misses.

'Fuck off!' I scream. 'That's not the issue is it? The issue is you've never really wanted to be a father and you're looking for an excuse to get out of it again. Fine then. Fuck off. If you're not going to be part of all this you can fuck off and leave.'

I stride into the kitchen and snatch the handset from its wall-mounted base.

'What are you doing?'

My fingers are shaking so much I have to hang up and redial twice.

She picks up on the fourth ring.

'Hi Mum,' I say. 'Guess what. I'm pregnant!'

Thursday February 10th
13 weeks and six days
183 days to go

Hi Bub,
This is your mum. Sorry I've taken so long.

Mark takes us via the back route. It's mainly farmland out here. We drive along narrow asphalt roads crumbling at the edges. Past green hectares of grazing land, neat lines of peach and cherry trees stretching up the hillsides, vast carpets of brussel sprouts and silverbeet. Occasionally a ute passes us going the other way, but mostly the road's all ours.

I've got my window down a crack, eye on the horizon, angling my face into the slipstream. Breakfast isn't sitting well and I'm feeling a little queasy.

The car slows. I glance at Mark as he turns us into a tight bend. The creases in his forehead are deeper than normal, the old chicken pox scar puckered into one of the folds. Eyebrows arched. Hazel almond eyes focused forward. Lips slightly parted, a clench of teeth in-between.

As the car straightens up our eyes meet.

'What?' There's a shaving nick under his jawline.

'Nothing.' I look away.

When we first met, almost twelve years ago, I thought Mark's jawline was his most physically attractive feature. Perhaps not in a classically handsome way. But for me there was something about it. In those early heady days I'd find myself staring at that jawline. In the dim light of movie screens, in the brighter light of restaurants. I loved its well defined angles. The way it animatedly moved during our long conversations over politics and the environment. The way it would dimple slightly when he smiled, dimple deeper when he laughed. And, after a respectable number of dates, the way it would twitch as he'd come.

These days Mark's jawline's much less well defined. It's slightly jowled, bordering on saggy. The dimples still occur when he laughs or smiles. It's just that now they seem to rarely happen.

I look out along the side of the road. At the never-ending stretch of barbed wire fence, the weeds in the ditch zooming past. I miss those dimples. The way they used to light up his face, the way they used to reach his eyes. When I think about it, not that I like to, but when I do, I know the truth. They slowed down, almost stopped, four years ago. Our annus horribilis.

My mind jerks away from that dangerous shard. I stare at a red tractor in the distance, count the clods flicking from the tyres, keep counting until it's out of sight. Anyway, it probably wasn't just that. There's times, especially after a particularly bad bout of arseholeness, that I suspect Mark's flares of panicky obsessiveness are part of his true underlying personality trait. That when we got together he was just wearing a happier, more relaxed mask. A mask that, eight years later, finally slipped off. It shouldn't be surprising really. Whether you agree with the nurture or nature side of the argument, all you need to do is look at Mark's dad.

Mark and Mr. Jackson.

Now that's a whole textbook of dysfunctional psychology on its own.

Another wave of nausea hits me. I wind the window down a bit more, chock the airvent towards me.

'Do we need to stop?' Mark's eyes flick between me and the road.

I shake my head.

'You sure?'

'I'm fine,' I say, a little annoyed at his mothering. 'Honestly.'

'Okay.' The car speeds up again.

I shouldn't complain. At least he's changed since those eight days. Those terrible eight days between when I heard the sonographer catch her breath and when I rang my mum. Those eight days I felt me and Bub were on our own. There's been all the massages, the cups of tea, the multivitamins lined up in the mornings. The file marked 'Pregnancy' I saw sitting on his desk. He's even started to clear out the nursery. It's almost like he's trying to overcompensate for his blip. To reassure me. And most of the time it works.

We pass a pair of weatherboard cottages facing each other on opposite sides of the road. Then a hedgerow on the right, a bored looking mare in the paddock. More houses now. A disused tennis court. The turnoff to Warburton highway coming up ahead.

There's times I worry though. It's hard to define. A certain tone that creeps into his voice, a certain hesitancy in his hugs, a certain something. Or maybe I'm just being paranoid.

My seatbelt tightens as we pull up at the stop sign. Mark checks both ways. We turn left.

All I know is that here we are.

Driving up to tell his parents the good news.

Two weeks after I told mine.

————————————————————

Steps to Remembrance

by Suvi Mahonen

It is a wet winter's weekday morning. Low grey clouds hide the top of the Mount Dandenong Ranges and a thin mist is drifting, making the surrounding trees seem ethereal. The windows are steamy and an oily sheen covers the road. I brace as we slow down and turn. Fine droplets of spray spin from the sides of the tyres as we pull into the Ferntree Gully Picnic Ground.

Getting out of the car with water bottle in hand I look around. Wide dull puddles lie across the asphalt. A stretch of damp grass slopes up from the car park to the edge of where the forest begins. All the picnic tables and barbecues seem empty and the education centre up the path appears closed. Clumps of breath form in front of my face in the icy mountainside air.

I shiver.

We're here to climb the 1000 Steps for our first time. We live relatively nearby and we've been meaning to for years, but the axiom of ignoring one's own backyard has applied. A recent visit to my GP, however, has finally shamed me into action.

The 1000 Steps/Kokoda Track Memorial Walk, located in the Dandenong Ranges National Park on the eastern outskirts of Melbourne, is a popular spot for exercise. Free Press Leader estimates over 54 000 people go on the walk each month. Local sports clubs often use it for training, and tour companies who take people on the real Kokoda Track in Papua New Guinea recommend the walk as a great way to build up fitness.

'Let's get moving,' my husband says. 'I can't feel my nose anymore.'

We head towards a stone archway that marks the beginning of the walk. Set into each pillar is a bronze plaque. One gives a brief history of the national park. The other contains a dedication to the Australian troops who fought on the Kokoda Track during World War II. I'm sobered to read that 625 soldiers died there.

We have to walk almost a kilometre up a dirt track before we get to the steps. Water bubbles beside us and crimson rosellas twitter in the trees. The ground slopes gently upwards and even though the air, if anything, is getting colder, I'm starting to warm up. Eventually the track opens into a small clearing, where, straight ahead, we see a set of narrow concrete steps heading up into the mountain. With a degree of naivety we take a swig from our water bottles and begin power-walking up them.

We enter into a tunnel of dimness created by the overhanging branches and thickening mist. Everything is wet. The blanket of ferns around us glistens, the trunks of the mountain ash gums are slick. We splash through puddles and squishy clumps of mud that have gathered in the centre depressions of the well-worn steps.

The steps ascend steeply, twisting left then right. Around us profuse growths of wattle, daisy bush and sassafras cover the mountainside. Tendrils of ivy twist up the furry stems of tree ferns and vines loop down towards the ground. It isn't long though before my appreciation of the surroundings is overtaken by the demands of my usually sedentary body. My thighs and calves protest first, then my hammering heart, then my oxygen-hungry lungs.

'Stop,' I call out.

My husband turns. His face is flushed. 'What?'

'I want to read this,' I pant, nodding at the bronze plaque next to me.

He descends the few steps and we read it together. It is titled 'Imita Ridge' and describes how, on that ridge in Papua New Guinea in September 1942, Australian troops had finally held off the advancing Japanese.

The plaque is one of thirteen that we come across on the walk. Each gives a brief history of a battle and a map of where it occurred on the Kokoda Track. Together they combine to tell the story of how the brave young Australian troops and their Papuan allies eventually defeated the Japanese. They are replicas of memorial plaques on the actual Kokoda Track and they were placed here along the 1000 Steps in 1997 because portions of this steep, bush-lined track are similar to the real track in Papua New Guinea.

I gaze into the thick dank forest behind the plaque and try to imagine how frightening it would be to know there could be an enemy sniper hiding in there.

After my pulse slows and my breathing steadies we keep going. I'm finding it a struggle. My legs ache, my throat burns, the tips of my ears and fingers go numb.

We stop at regular intervals to read the plaques and catch our breaths. Around us the spread of temperate rainforest stretches away into misty oblivion. People of various shades of fitness pass us, going up and down.

After half an hour of climbing the mountain ash and manna gums start to thin. The steps gradually become wider and less steep. But just when I think the track is coming to an end it turns sharply and keeps heading up. The sight of another stretch sends my muscles into rebellion. I step off the path and stop at a small divet in the dirt bank.

'What's the matter?' my husband asks.

'What do you think?' I say. I'm bent over double, panting like a pack horse.

I straighten and wince as a stitch hits me. Giant dark green fern fronds hang overhead, their undersides pebbled with tiny drops of condensation. Below us, behind a massive moss-covered hollowed-out log, I can hear the sound of steady footsteps and someone else's harsh breathing.

A tall thin white-haired man comes around the corner and into view. He's going at a brisk pace, almost jogging. As he gets closer I notice the deep lines in his weathered face.

'Don't worry guys,' he says to us as he passes. 'You're almost there.'

'Great,' my husband mutters as we watch the man's back heading up the steps. 'Now we've been overtaken by someone almost twice our age.'

'I don't care,' I say. 'I don't think I can go any further.'

'Don't be silly,' my husband says. 'We're not turning around now.'

'Piggyback me,' I plead.

He laughs.

I sigh, grab the handrail, and lever myself forward. To our right the bank is covered with kangaroo ferns and dogwood, to our left it falls away into the thickets of a gully. We pass a big boulder cobbled with blue lichen and green moss. And then, finally, beyond the highest step and between the trunks of box gums, I can see the edge of a clearing.

'Thank goodness,' I say. I turn and give my husband a high five.

On shaky legs I stumble up the last few steps and flop down on a rock. For several minutes I'm too busy regaining my breath and chugging down what's left of my water to notice my surroundings. When I do, I see the white-haired man doing thigh squats by a bench. There's half a dozen other people up here as well, resting, milling about, everyone looking pleased with themselves.

The clearing itself is nothing spectacular. Just a smallish flat patch of land with a couple of benches. There's no sign saying we've reached the top of the 1000 Steps and any panoramic view of Melbourne is hidden by the surrounding trees. On the opposite side there's a fenced-off pond and two dirt roads heading further up the mountain.

I go over to see if I can spot any frogs. I'm sticky with sweat and my hair's a mess. A girl in her early twenties is standing by the fence. Dressed in a purple windcheater and black leggings she looks totally relaxed, like someone who's only just walked to the mailbox and back.

'Do you do this walk often?' I ask her.

Her name is Amber and it turns out she does. 'Three or four times a week,' she says. She tells me she's a university student. 'Coming here is a lot cheaper than going to the gym and it's a great way to keep fit.'

Not being at all fit myself, I don't trust my legs and we decide to return via the Lyrebird Track. It's longer but less steep and contains no steps. As we walk, I threaten my husband with resolutions of a new shared exercise regime.

When we get back down we wander past the playground where two children are squealing in delight as they run around the swings. A couple in their sixties are minding them nearby. They smile at us and say hello. I ask if they're planning to take the children up the steps.

The man's moustache lifts as he laughs.

'No,' he says. 'We're just here on a playground outing with the grandkids.'

His name is Alan Grubb, and he's a retired engineer. He's wearing a tan wind parka and silver-rimmed glasses and is happy to start up a conversation. We quickly discover this place holds a deeper significance for him.

His uncle, Will Sanders, was a soldier in the Australian 39th Militia Battalion during World War II. He was killed on the Kokoda Track at the age of nineteen. Alan becomes animated as he tells us about the gruelling conditions the 39th Battalion experienced when they were sent up the Kokoda Track to face the advancing Japanese.

'The army was desperate,' he says. 'They rounded up a bunch of mainly eighteen and nineteen year olds and shipped them there with hardly any training. Most of these kids had never left Victoria before. Next thing they know they're in the middle of the jungle with barely any supplies and not enough ammunition.'

Alan's mother used to come to this park in memory of her brother. Alan believes it is important to have a memorial park like this for the relatives of the fallen, as well as to help educate younger Australians about what happened on the Kokoda Track during a time in our country's history when the country's fate hung in balance.

After we talk a while we thank Alan for sharing his connection to this place with us and head back to our car. Before we get there we stop at the picnic ground's flag poles. In front of them are three plaques commemorating the heroic deeds of the 14th, 16th and 39th Australian Infantry Battalions during the Kokoda campaign.

A flock of sulphur-crested cockatoos are feeding on the grass nearby, and the clouds are starting to break, allowing dapples of sunlight to come through. A sense of gratitude fills me that these soldiers were willing to risk everything so that us future generations of Australians could enjoy peace like this.

On our drive home I think back to our walk and feel ashamed of the complaints I'd made. I knew it couldn't compare to what those young men had been through.

Fever

by Kate McGonigle

If I tell you how much I like fevers and their paths through my children, will you think me mad? The hot sweet flush of the boys' cheeks, the proof of a battle waged. Microscopic navy seals lash themselves to uboats and comb the seas for mines, dealing with the mythical snakes of the sea, all in the space of a limp child body- the last great patriotic act?

There is a cycle to the illness, the role I play as mother and know-it-all-- or utter make-believe mom. Whoever taught me how to care for sick kids, why am I expected to know what to do?! It is only now, six years into the game, that I *almost* know what to do. Almost. My role radically changes though as the illness draws out, expands, contracts and dominates the familiar world. This time around we seem to be on a 5 day cycle, looping around at least twice. RinseWashRepeat.

It has been a week and a half of sick kids, and I'm just barely coming out of the caretake, just barely sentient. But there is work being done, and growth still happening, so thrive we will. Today is Day 10 of someone of the four of us being down for the count with what is now a vague malaise, fever just enough to cause a flush and a chill (the delirium tremens being a shake that proves work is being done), a rosy eye-lid and an inability to sleep well or deeply, or in one's own bed. The limbs of boys at 4 AM do multiply. How can there be so many, so everywhere? An extra blanket, an irrational chill and the body does its glorious dance of healing itself. Some wild body-need for growth, for a purging to set the scene for the second half, the culmination of the bawdy action that started out on a cleared stage. As I tire, there is less all-knowing pretend-mother behavior and more practicality, more conservation of energy. Shorter sentences. Wash the towels, just the towels. Dry them. Place them over the sofa cushions, and on the floor next to the sofas. Put them on the beds. Conserve, conserve your energy. Make tea, get honey, ask for help, get groceries dropped off, eggs every night. Eggs are a miracle of efficiency, protein, poetically bland, smooth on a sore throat. Eggs.

The day after, that first night of cool sleep, cold sweat on the brow. However many days it took to get there, there is an immediate sense of blessing that the moment of crisis is passed/past. I think sometimes, even during the event, that I can see its end or envision the morning clearly, but nothing beats that first good night. Whatever and Whatever may be Coming, but there is a really clear relief once the worry lets up and 'normal' is in sight. The 'really clear relief' is mixed with a muddy adrenalin comedown, a simmer and a stew, sometimes in the same hour. Resentment, a *don't I wish I could actually use the babysitter we had coming, but no!* or a *it would be nice if someone else could do the vomit laundry*. A re-assertion of the memories of all the mothering failures, a depression of an aggressively passive sort- if that makes sense.

Then there is the day after that, normality is more in-reach but not quite in the room. The windows are clean, you can see the sun outside. Nobody feels well, but no one is talking about it anymore. . .
Then there is the day after that. Apologies have been made to the sickness gods, children have been restored innocence in the destruction of their mother's life, husbands have returned to the living. And now comes the insanity of post-reconstruction.

And then- at least here- it all starts again. There will be laundry, lots of laundry. I have stopped talking for the most part and am hoping the massive honey dosing that I am administering will help me carry the boat through the water this week, but I am weakened and in this weakness, I don't see health on the horizon, but exhaustion. Deep, deep exhaustion, as step one in the ladder leading to the morning after, the next hot mess of a Family Life.

Escapes

by Tony Wayne Brown

Blood-red bugs crawled out of Chacun Wayne's gaping mouth as his body-shattered like a windshield that has exploded from the heat of a scorching summer sun-lay scattered on the sand that marked the Jicarilla Apache reservation's edge. The young hitchhiker almost appeared to be sleeping, hidden in a depression amid a thick clump of sagebrush next to a pinon tree that bordered Route 44.

The crumpled form remained as still as the New Mexico air above. Tousled sun-bleached hair tumbled to the burning sand as empty sockets which once held eyes stared at the relentless rays of an eternal August day.

Fragments of a car's headlight marked the crushed chest of the frozen figure, where the naked red head of a black turkey vulture was hard at work. All around the body, hundreds of large red ants ran in circular races, fighting for their fair share of the spoils. A battered and bruised right hand stretched out from the corpse in the direction of a blue barrel cactus, as if beckoning for a drink of water from its interior reservoir long after there was any need for it. Chacun would never be thirsty again.

He would never be hurt again, either.

The sadistic Jeep driver who'd given him a ride, then done such terrible things to him far off the road, couldn't hurt him. The father who'd beaten him so often the past twelve years couldn't hurt him. Not even the gossipers back home in Albuquerque could hurt him now. No longer would the boy overhear snatches of whispered conversations about the death of his beloved mother.

Chacun Wayne was forever free.

The vulture knew Chacun's death immediately. It had been patiently waiting above for two days while the 16-year-old struggled back to the road that bisected northwestern New Mexico. The persistent scavenger kept its vigil as day turned to night. It had watched as the exhausted traveler below fell asleep. The bird hadn't known that it was a nightmarish sleep or that the same horrid scene that had haunted the boy's sleep for so many years had become clear in meaning for the first time.

The vision of his mother's body flying past him at the top of the stairs as she reached out to save him from falling, only to tumble to death herself down the black metal stairwell, had now come to his consciousness. Something still tugged at the corner of his mind, telling him that the whole story was yet to be revealed, but it refused to emerge from the shadows of his mind. The bird eying him now from far above as Chacun struggled to remember was only following its instinct, awaiting the feast that the inevitable would bring.

When the approaching sedan had awakened the boy from the deep dream about his mother's tragic death a dozen years before, the gliding bird just bided its time. It had no way of conceiving Chacun's feeling of dread when he'd realized who was driving the car that was approaching in the middle of the night, in the middle of the desert. The bird didn't know that there was no way the tortured youth would allow himself to be dragged back into the torment of a life replete with constant fear and pain.

Watching as the noisy Monte Carlo sped closer to the hitchhiker below, the coolly dispassionate scavenger hadn't blinked at all when the boy suddenly flung himself into the Chevrolet's path. The vulture recognized death when the body flew into the air and off the arrow-straight stretch of asphalt though. It knew the look of death because death was its way of life.

The driver had also recognized death at once. Like the vulture, he'd seen it before. The tall man with a large gut sitting behind the steering wheel didn't even momentarily hesitate. Visions of another death long ago were all he saw. He only shook his long brown hair, kept his foot on the gas pedal, and continued on his way toward the Jicarilla Apache reservation. More than ever, Wallace Wayne needed to find his son Chacun to start making up for all the grief he had caused over the years. An empty envelope with the return address of his son's grandfather was the sole clue as to where he might have headed after he'd run away.

Miles had passed since the collision, but Wallace couldn't stop shaking. He kept telling himself it was just a wild animal, but even in his mental condition he knew that wasn't true. The car's raucous muffler continued to shatter the night as miles and miles rolled by; the body left behind was forgotten as the car erratically wove down the lonely stretch of blacktop.

Taking a long swig from a nearly empty fifth of Jack Daniels, Wallace felt as if he were going to pass out. He finally slowed the car. Seeing a hard-packed area where he could get the Chevy off the road without getting stuck in sand, he steered off the asphalt and parked behind a thin cover of tumbleweed and ponderosa pines. Blooming for the first time in 15 years, a century plant stood six-feet-tall near the car, with its flowering cap and ramrod straightness reminding him of a Buckingham Palace guard he'd once seen in London. Its beauty somehow gave him solace in the cold night air.

Sitting in the baleful calm of the quiet desert, with only an occasional series of three hoots from a barred owl and a lone coyote's howl to break the silence, Wallace remembered the day his beloved Mourning Dove died. Thoughts of her and what she'd tried to do to her own son filtered through the alcoholic haze as his panicked mind searched incessantly for sanity.

'Why did she feel she had to do it?' he whispered to the century plant, thinking of the night his wife died at the base of the curving wrought-iron stairwell of their stucco split-level home in Albuquerque. It was that damned night that had led him to where he was now...in the middle of nowhere, chasing the past that he had driven away...chasing a dream that had died long ago.

After he'd finally sobered up long enough to decide to look for his runaway son at the reservation, things had gotten worse. Even though Wallace was determined to overcome the vengeful senseless feelings harbored within him toward his son ever since Dove died, his willpower had failed him again. He hadn't been able to pass by the flashing red-and-green neon 'Beer' sign lighting up the front picture window of that old tavern.

Why didn't I just ask if anybody'd seen Chacun?

Wallace stared and stared at the stately ponderosas guarding the parked Monte Carlo. He'd known exactly what was going to happen even before walking inside that creaky bar in Little Cuba. As soon as he'd entered the smoky, dimly-lit redneck watering hole with the stuffed elk's head over the bar and had seen the perspiring necks of the brown beer bottles in the cowboys' rough hands...the rows of liquor bottles lining the shelves behind the scarred wooden counter...the cold, golden liquid freely flowing, he'd realized he couldn't withstand the terrible urge which had held him captive for so many years.

The barred owl hooted again, sounding closer. Wallace rolled down the car's windows as far as they'd go, hoping the frigid night air would make his mind go blank, but it didn't. Taking another swill that emptied the bottle, the pathetic figure said, "That's where my problems began." What he was referring to had no connection to the body left behind on Route 44, but to that event so long ago that had changed his life--and Chacun's.. His obsession with that moment had ruined both their lives. Only death could get the look in Dove's eyes out of his mind.

Slumped on the front seat, Wallace failed to see the stars fading. Falling into an uncomfortable sleep, he dozed fitfully for many hours until it was nighttime again. When he finally woke up as the stars brightened, his sense of time had lost the day. He opened another bottle and chugged almost half of it before replacing the cap. A U.S. Army Reserve convoy of desert-colored semi's pulling low-boy trailers loaded with M-1 tanks and armored personnel carriers paraded by and Wallace, a veteran Vietnam War tank jockey, saluted as best he could. He'd never been ashamed to have fought on behalf of freedom from oppression, no matter how much the long-hairs had jeered him when he came off the C-130 transport in San Diego, where he would muster out a changed man.

Fighting for what's right is never wrong, he thought. What happened to me? How'd I get like this?

No answer came.

With a new burst of determination, he slapped himself hard on the cheek to try and sober up, but it didn't do much good. He started the Monte Carlo's engine, pulled back onto Route 44 and quickly got the worn-out car up to a high speed. Just a bare sliver of moon shone overhead as the Chevy ran off the road, then narrowly swerved past a fennec fox which had left its daytime burrow to chase lizards. After Wallace barely managed to regain control of the vehicle, his mind went back to visions of his black-haired woman--the way she looked before hitting her head on the terrazzo floor at the bottom of the stairs. Her brown eyes had reflected the same wild spark he'd seen just as briefly in the fox's eyes when the car's only

functioning headlight spotlighted the startled animal.

As the sedan advanced toward the reservation, swaying from side to side--once barely missing a passing Taos Trucking 18-wheeler--Wallace Wayne's mind drifted back to the past once more. He recalled the prominent cheekbones which displayed Dove's kinship to the defiant Jicarilla warrior Chacun, who had not gained notoriety among the white faces, only because he was more crafty than others like Geronimo and Cochise of the nearby Chiricahua Apaches. She had always wished that he'd been like Chacun, who fought unceasingly for what he believed in.

He was a hero to his own people, and that was all that had mattered to her.

Thinking back of the unspoken desperation apparent in her gazes for many months before her death, tears fell from Wallace's eyes this time though for how his own life might have been.

He'd failed her. That's all he could think as the one-eyed Chevy cut through the night. When he'd finally understood how the alien confusion of a big city and the burden of a demanding child had not been part of a young girl's dreams who had fled her reservation for the bright city lights, he should have done something about it instead of just assuming it was just a passing phase.

Hunched over the steering wheel, Wallace began speeding up and slowing down, responding rhythmically to his twisted memories. Days ago in Albuquerque, when his only child walked out and slammed the screen door behind him, he hadn't even been able to get out of his easy chair because he was too drunk. He'd only screamed, 'What's the matter with you? You anxious to die, boy?' instead of reaching out with the love he'd buried in spite so long ago. Even if he had tried to catch his son before he could leave it only would have resulted again in more bruises for Chacun...for his precious son, who had never done the first thing to deserve such a fate.

Why? Why? Why?

Speeding up once more, this time pushing the pedal to the floor, Wallace forced the car up to 90. Shaking like a battered boxer after way too many bouts, the old engine threw out warning steam and threatened to blow, but he was in such a feverish desire to find his son that he didn't notice the rods knocking. He had to tell Chacun the secret cause for his agony since he'd been four. Wallace wished he'd told him the truth long ago--the whole truth. It just was not that simple, though.

How do you tell your only child he was the reason his own mother died?

That question had chased Wallace over the years, but he'd never found a satisfactory solution. When Dove blamed her baby boy for keeping her trapped at home and ruining her night life, he'd dismissed it as the short-lived frustration of a harassed young mother.

Since that awful August evening almost twelve years ago, when Wallace had found out exactly how deep those feelings of frustrations were, his soul had been dead. The split-second vision of Dove trying to push Chacun off the second-floor balcony had destroyed her loving husband's heart. From that time on, Wallace's deluded mind always managed to find someone other than himself or her to blame.

For all those years, he held a grainy slow-motion black-and-white view of his wife plunging down the wrought-iron lined steps after Chacun dodged, thinking it was all just the normal game he and his mother had often played when her depression was on hiatus. In the torment of a grieving husband and lover, the focus for his misguided anger was the person least to blame...Chacun, an innocent child who was not responsible for his mother's overwhelming, illogical despair.

The pace began to take its toll on the '72 Chevy's engine, and the rods began knocking even louder, bringing Wallace back into the present. Slowing the car a bit, the bleary-eyed driver persisted in his urgent dash to the home of Chacun's grandfather, a revered medicine man and counselor of his tribe. Not knowing what lay behind, not knowing what would lie ahead, Wallace felt that the demon who had taken over his mind the day she died signified his failure not only as a husband and father, but as a man.

"Why did I wait so long to go after him?" he muttered, all the while knowing liquor once again had made him unable to function on that day, the same as this day. I've got to become a real man again...a real father. God take me away if I ever hurt my boy again!

"Things are gonna get better now...you wait and see!" he yelled, waving a clenched first at a turkey vulture looking for a meal. The sun rose in the sky, mottled with a pinkish-gray hue and spotty black patches of storm clouds to the east. He took the half-empty liquor bottle from between his legs, and whirled to toss it onto the back seat. His eyes engorged when they focused on the road ahead again, seeing the Chevy headed straight for a large boulder on the shoulder of the road. Wildly overcorrecting, he steered the car into a skid across the pavement and it smashed through a guard rail, plummeting backwards down a ravine cut into the rock bed by flood waters eons ago. His eyes fixated on the bird of death watching him from the sky--knowing this time it was his own demise that would be observed.

The vulture gracefully dipped its wing and dove to earth. The sun reached its zenith, then faded into night. The terror of knowing death remained welded in the dead man's eyes until they were there no more. Crumpled and torn among the harshness of the rocky ravine floor, he would never drink another drop of whisky or beer. He would never hurt anyone again. His pain was gone as well. No more whispered accusations overheard in the grocery store, whispers blaming him, whispers accusing him, whispers he refused to end by revealing the horrible truth of her death. They wouldn't have believed him, anyway.

With two more dawns came the revolving lights of the New Mexico State Patrol after a rattlesnake hunter had reported the wreck. The scavenger that had patiently waited above, and a half-dozen more that had joined it for a meal, scattered in all directions. Two troopers frowned as they peered at an all-too-familiar sight.

'Least he didn't take nobody with him,' one trooper said as they examined the crushed and torn corpse, which was lying halfway through the windshield on the Monte Carlo's hood, in the midst of a black cloud of flies recently born of maggots. The almost completely severed right hand lay on the car's hood, with the fingers nearly touching the remnants of the right headlight.

'Almost looks like he was callin' for help, don't it?' the other trooper said from behind a pair of silver-framed Foster Grant sunglasses. He wrapped his arms tightly to his chest to keep from shuddering.

The sockets that once held the dead man's eyes stared at the eternal summer sun, incapable of seeing what he had done--not in this human form at least. The broken headlight and the splattered drops of blood on it went unnoticed, and a half-full bottle of Jack Daniels only told half the tale as blood-red bugs crawled out of Wallace Wayne's gaping mouth.

Still Life With Limbs

Asleep beneath her knees every night
I should draw little mountaineers on them
Some Lilliputian adventurers
Conquering those boney fleshy peaks
Amidst the sands of Fire Island
Three thousand miles away
Where the surf is troubled
And the horseshoe crabs come to die
Under the mooning, star full, cloud gone sky

I should wave goodbye

I can get these things from some other place
The barbequed beer in the butt chicken
The shrimpy blinis
Margaritas or Pimms or
Dirty Martinis
The fires at night
The dog hair at dawn
The cardinals and grackles
But never piping plovers
Nestled in the no go dune

The blown jobs
The hot foot
The boats in the bay
The bobbing along
The going home

They can be found
Or recreated in Greece or Ibiza
I am not tied to this
Strip of sand
But you in that photograph
Your knees being bronzed
Are forever stranded

Anthony Murphy

Another Year Wiser

by Kim Rock

1st Birthday

The mommy and daddy brought home a brand new baby to their 5 year old daughter, who had a commonplace name that didn't quite fit her beautiful face. They didn't want to make the same mistake twice (assuming the good genes would continue on), so they thought long and hard of a name for the new girl that was sure to stand out. The mommy created the first name herself, and took the middle name from a pop-culture icon, often viewed as an American sex symbol due to her overwhelming beauty. The last name came from the daddy, of course, but it was definitely no small addition.

Would a rose by any other name still really smell as sweet?

They called her "cutie-beauty" for a while, just to make sure it would stick.

It's not like there were any high expectations or anything.

7th Birthday

The mommy would take the girl to the pet store and she'd press her nose up against the glass window. The girl told anyone who would listen, "I'm going to be a veterinarian so I can play with animals all day. I'll make them better when they're sick, so they'll never be sad."

Because she was seven, nobody ever bothered to tell her that's not the way the world works.

But today, this day, would be a day of all days. Today the mommy promised her she would get a kitten that would be all her own. It would love her and cuddle her and never leave her. It would need her.

She was so excited she could barely sleep the night before. Well, that and the screaming coming from the room below. But she had pretty much gotten used to that.

As the day grew longer she was losing hope, because the mommy didn't always do what she said she would. Sometimes the mommy would forget, or fall asleep, or change her mind. Which made the girl mad, because aren't mommies supposed to do what they say and keep their promises? The mommy wasn't good with promises, but she certainly made a lot.

The mommy ran a bath for herself and asked the girl, as usual, to bring her a glass of wine. This made her excited because once the mommy was finished she would finally get dressed and the girl would get her kitten, after all. But each time the mommy finished a glass she asked for a new one, until she stopped asking.

The girl found her asleep in the tub and even after she drained the water, the mommy wouldn't get out. When the sister was able to drag the mommy to the bedroom, there was some screaming and yelling and scolding, but no getting dressed. The lights went out and the girl knew that marked the end of another day, and she would just have to try again tomorrow.

10th Birthday

The girl sat on the edge of the squeaky hotel room bed, while the sister chain-smoked on the balcony, just ahead outside the open doorway.

"Where could they be? It's been hours, this is getting fucking ridiculous." The sister shot a look to her boyfriend indicating that her question was, indeed, rhetorical. No need for smart remarks at a time like this. He shrugged and the girl continued to rub the smooth stone he'd given her earlier, a present from one of the shops on the boardwalk. "It's a stress stone," he said, "so when you're feeling scared or upset, you can hold it tight and things will seem a little better."

The girl could feel it in the air, that familiar tension building up to something bad, explosive even. Like when the daddy's face would get beet red and he would start screaming out of nowhere, she had to be careful to avoid saying the things which would trigger him. "Walking on eggshells," the sister called it, but the girl thought it was more like walking on broken glass. Her whole life was a minefield.

The sister peered over the edge and squinted her eyes to see into the night, "Okay, I think I see mom walking up now... who are those guys helping her? Great, she and dad aren't together, just great." The girl thought about how the mommy and daddy never kissed anymore or even looked at each other.

When the mommy finally made it back to the room she was falling all over the place, speaking incoherent babble. "Look at the lake girls! It's s-s-o beautiful, sparkly, shiny. Let's go for a shwim!" She started pulling at the sister's clothes and was smacked away.

"Don't touch me! Get the fuck off of me, you're drunk! You're always drunk and you're killing yourself. You'll probably kill us too and I can't fucking take this anymore!" The sister wrestled with the mommy until she was able to lock her in the bathroom. That was the first time the girl ran away.

A few months later as the mommy stopped at a red light, she turned her head around to smile at the girl in the backseat, "How would you like it if you, your sister and I got our own place to stay away from dad? A special place for just the three of us." The girl smiled back just as big and nodded in excitement. The mommy turned her head and said to the sister, "Wow, that was easier than I thought" and the girl wondered what about that could be bad.

12th Birthday

The girl held her two-week old nephew in her arms for the first time. He was so small she knew if she dropped him he would shatter into a thousand pieces. She didn't know what to say or do; this small being rendered her helpless in its own helplessness and that terrified her.

"Now, don't go getting any ideas," the mother cooed, her voice was gentle for the baby, but her eyes were serious, desperate even. It was then the girl realized this would now be the expectation she would have to outlast, make it another five years without getting knocked up and then, maybe, you can have your identity back. But lucky for the girl she never liked to do what people expected. She always liked to prove them wrong.

15th Birthday

The father and the girl sat at a table for four in the corner of the restaurant, the same seafood chain they had been going to for the past few years. It was their unspoken agreement that he would pay for dinner and she would eat as fast as she could, because it was not often they were subjected to spending long, uninterrupted periods of time together. And that was the way she liked it.

They were now waiting on the sister and the nephew who were, of course, late. The girl had mentally prepared herself for this though, as lateness seemed to be a genetic trait the girl and the sister both shared. A curse passed along from their mother, no doubt. But the father was not quite as understanding and getting more irritable by the minute. The longer they waited the more agonizing it became and the air was getting so thick that, finally, the girl suggested they leave. On the drive home sheets of rain coated the windows.

About twenty minutes after they had returned home and fled to their separate corners of the house, the phone's shrill ring pierced her ears and it clicked: *something was horribly wrong.*

At the hospital, the mother hadn't yet arrived. The girl and the father were taken to the nephew first, who had been conscious when the ambulance arrived. He informed everyone what had happened, "Mommy crashed her car in the rain."

The girl walked into a room in ICU and saw a stranger stuffed with tubes, torn clothes, chest barely rising. She heard the doctors' diagnoses repeating over and over, "...deflated lung, cracked pelvis, four broken ribs, severe bodily trauma..." The girl collapsed to the floor in heaps and sobs. She didn't return until eight days later, when the sister was moved to the recovery wing. The girl couldn't allow herself to watch her only family die.

17th Birthday

The girl looked out onto the French Riviera, with the dazzling sun shining off water so blue it was like dancing in the sky. The beach was mostly pebbles and her feet were still numb hours afterward, but she could have stayed there for days on end, watching the tide come in, only sea and sky for miles and miles.

She had spent all her money, but what she did have was laughter, the stars, and too much French wine (if there is such a thing). She stumbled back to the hotel room when the sun was just returning over the horizon, cheeks as pink as the sky. She laid there and thought of the previous eleven days which encompassed her first European excursion and how she would begin the journey home in just a few short hours.

And then she puked.

18th Birthday

The girl felt her pocket buzz and reached down to pull out her phone. The name of the caller read "Father." She sent it to voicemail. She hadn't spoken to him since he failed to show up to her graduation and couldn't think of a reason why she would ever want to again. She had already received a call from her grandparents; they sang to her as they did every year and made sure she had received their check. Then came a text from her mother, "Happy Birthday Cutey Beauty", with a slew of emoticons. Digital love. The sister had confirmed she wouldn't be able to attend dinner; she was under the weather and her hips were sore from the rain. The girl was weary of the obligations, couldn't help but be disappointed when they were ultimately not upheld.

She thought she would be better off without celebrating anymore birthdays, but she kept getting older.

◆———————————◆

BETTER BOOBS

by Mark Barkawitz

"How do you like my new boob, Mike?" Kelly smiled as I approached her on the front porch of her Sierra Madre cottage. She stuck her left one forward for me to inspect. It was impossible to detect any difference under her sweater and bra.

"Looks good to me." I'm a painting contractor, mostly residential, so I tend to work for a lot of women on their homes. I drink a lot of coffee and talk a lot. Sometimes, they confide in me. Last year, just as I was putting the finishing touches on Kelly's kitchen remodel she was diagnosed with breast cancer. Her sister had died a few years ago of the same thing. Kelly had gone through a lot in the year since I'd seen her: mastectomy, chemo, radiation, recovery, and finally, her new boob. We hugged.

"You look good, kid."

"Thanks. I feel good." She smiled again. "Gary likes it, too." Gary was her husband.

I laughed. I do that a lot too. We went inside. She poured me a cup of coffee. I leaned against the counter, sipped her strong, hot brew, and we gabbed for the next hour or so about everything except cancer. We finally got around to scheduling a starting date for some touch-ups around the house. I put my empty coffee cup in her sink.

"You have another job to go to today?" she asked.

"Yup. Or I'd let you feed me, too." She was a good cook. We both laughed. Kelly did that a lot too. Probably why we got along so well.

"Next time," she said.

We hugged goodbye and I hurried out to my truck, where I'd left my cell phone on the seat. One missed call. I recognized the number; it was the Waters', my next job. I called back.

"Haylo?" It was the housekeeper's voice.

"Mariela?"

"Si. Is that you, Mikey?"

"Si."

"Mar-rgo wants to know if you still coming today?" Margo Waters was the homeowner. It had been a few months since I'd last worked at the Waters' Castle, as I called it. It was an old, two-and-a-half story, twenty-eight room, concrete-walled, multi-million-dollar mansion on Pasadena's west side above the arroyo overlooking the Rose Bowl. I painted one room seven years ago and had worked there doing odd jobs on-and-off ever since.

"I'm on my way. Did you miss me?"

"Oh, si. You so nice. You always help Mariela." I carried groceries up the back stairs for her, nothing any gentleman wouldn't do for a lady. No big deal.

"I have sooprise," she said.

"For me?"

"No, ees not for you. But ees sooprise."

A few minutes later, I turned into the long driveway that led back to the Castle. I parked, grabbed a few hand tools I figured I'd need, and headed up the back stairway. Through the row of kitchen windows on the landing, I saw Mariela inside at the sink. I knocked on the door but opened it myself.

"Morning."

"Hi, Mikey. Coffee ees in microwave for you." She continued to wash dishes in the sink. "Mar-rgo go to gym. Leave note for you." Without turning towards me, she indicated with a nod it was on the island.

I turned on the microwave, checked the note. I recognized Margo's handwriting:

-fix latch on cab in Butler's Pantry

-paint walls in Guest Room

"Margo's sister went home?"

"Si."

"How is she?"

Mariela shook her head. "Ees no good. Berry sick."

I nodded. Margo's sister was currently going through what Kelly had gone through last year. But Margo's sister had been pregnant at the time the cancer was discovered, which had delayed and complicated her treatment, and the cancer had spread. The oven dinged. I took out the cup, sipped the steamy coffee, went back to the list:

-replace all burnt-out light bulbs

-move potted trees from east patio to west patio

-assemble automatic cat box

"Automatic cat box?"

"Si. Mar-rgo get a new kitty."

"Really?" In all the time I'd worked in the Castle, the Waters had never had a pet. From under the island, a black paw reached out for my shoelace. I put down the cup, got down on one knee and bent low. Yellow-green, almond-shaped eyes stared back at me from the jet black face of a young feline—too old to be a kitten, too young to be a cat—perched like a sphinx, ready to pounce. "Hey, there." I

reached in to pet its head between ears pointed upright. "What's it's name?"

"Hair-rball."

"'Hairball?' That's funny. How you doing, Hairball?" It purred gently. Then I noticed each nail on its front paws was coated with some kind of clear, plastic sheath. I took its paw in my hand to inspect it more closely. "What the heck?"

Still at the sink, Mariela looked down. "Ees so kitty won't scratch furniture."

"You're kidding." I ran my fingers across the floor in front of Hairball, who reached out to spoke my hand with its paw. The soft, acrylic sheaths kept its fingernails from digging into the skin on the back of my hand. I had to laugh. "What will they think of next?" Then I remembered the list—"-assemble automatic cat box"—and figured I'd find out soon enough.

"How's you knee?" Mariela asked.

"Not bad. Rehab took awhile, but I'm back up to five or six miles a run now." I'd hurt it last summer. Didn't know how. Just woke up one morning and out of nowhere the darn thing was swollen like a volleyball. I sipped the coffee and found the loose latch in the adjoining pantry, took the Phillips screwdriver from my back pocket and carefully tightened the guilty, loose screw heads. "How's your back?" I asked through the doorway.

"Oh, ees bueno. I'm so glad. I tell Mar-rgo ees no more heavy lifting." She had been wearing a brace because of a lower back strain, but it was hard to tell under her baggy sweatshirt if she was still wearing it. She dried her hands on the dishtowel, turned to me with a funny, conspiratorial sort of look on her face. "You remember what we talk about last time you are here?"

I thought back.

"Come on." She prodded me. "You remember." She smiled and winked.

"Oh." I did suddenly remember—breast implants. Mariela had lost thirty pounds over the last year-and-a half but had confessed to being unhappy with how the weight-loss had left her breasts, so she had consulted a plastic surgeon in the San Fernando valley. I glanced down slightly, but the loose-fitting sweatshirt hid any clear indication. So risking a faux pas, I was compelled to ask uneasily: "Did you do it?"

She pursed her lips and nodded.

"Really?" I looked again. More closely. "Obviously, you didn't opt for the Ds." Her husband's suggestion, as I remembered.

"No." She shook her head. "Ees a full C."

"Ahh. A full C."

"You want to see?"

"What?"

"Come on. I show you." She walked ahead of me farther into the house. I followed—what else could I do?—through the dining room, where from a wall-sized painting the luminous faces of Renaissance men and women stared judgmentally down at me, into a small hallway. She closed the doors at both ends. She turned to me and pulled up the baggy sweatshirt, under which firm, twin mounds—like cantaloupe halves—were wrapped snug by a cotton crop top.

"Oh." I couldn't help staring. But didn't figure it rude in this instance anyway.

"Ees no bra," she stated proudly.

"No, bra? You're kidding?"

She shook her head. "No. Ees too sensitive." She covered them up again, smiled again. "Eh?"

"To quote my favorite sitcom: 'They're spectacular.' Good for you. Good for your husband, too," I kidded.

"Oh, he crazy now. He keep asking doctor: 'How soon? How soon?'"

"So you haven't tried them out yet?"

"No, no, no." She wagged her index finger like a mother playfully instructing a child. "Ees too sensitive. Doctor say ees okay for Saturday night."

"Really?" I smiled, thinking of her husband. "This Saturday?"

She nodded, wagged her finger at me again. "Doan you tell no one. Ees secret. No want Mar-rgo to know. I tell her I have back surgery. Take two weeks off. Thees morning she look over while I cook. But I no tell her."

"Yeah, she might get pissed off now that her housekeeper has better boobs." We both laughed.

A door closed with a thud from the kitchen end of the house.

"Ees Mar-rgo. I go now." She hurried out the doorway towards the kitchen. I knew she'd clean-up my half-finished coffee cup on the way.

I went the other direction, up the stairs to the guest room, where the pillows were perfectly arranged on the bed and the bedspread was pulled snuggly across the mattress—not a wrinkle to indicate a human being had ever slept there. The blue walls didn't really need patching or painting, but Margo quite often changed colors on a whim—sometimes her own, sometimes her interior decorator's. A paint chip card was scotch-taped to the wall; the soft yellow color was named: "Morning." I took the flat-head screwdriver from my back pocket and began removing the brass faceplates, putting them all together in an empty wastebasket. A few minutes later, Margo poked her head in the room. "Hi, Mike."

"Hey, Margo. How goes it?"

"Okay." But she sounded weary, not convincing. She wore a designer work-out jacket and pants. Had recently turned forty, but was quite fit and attractive. A personal trainer at the gym and the Wonder bra under her little, white T-shirt helped.

"Sister moved back home. Huh?"

She nodded. "Yeah. She and the kids left last week." They had been staying with Margo during her sister's treatment at the USC-Norris Cancer Center.

"How is she?"

She shrugged her shoulders. "It's too early to tell." Sounding like a doctor, she educated me on the billions of cancer cells that had made up the multiple tumors that had forced the removal of both breasts, then maximum chemo and radiation treatments. Her sister's hair had fallen out. She had lost twenty-five pounds.

Trying to give Margo some hope, I told her about Kelly and her new boob.

"That's nice. But it won't save your friend if the cancer comes back."

I got more stuff from the truck, covered the furniture with plastic and the carpet with drop cloths. I'd paint the walls tomorrow. Change-out the lights and assemble the automatic cat box, too. Today, tomorrow? What the hell did it matter? I didn't see Margo or Mariela on my way out. But it was a big house. You could get lost. So in the kitchen, I wrote a note on the island to let them know I'd be back first thing tomorrow. From under the island, the black paw reached out for my pant leg, but its prophylactic nails couldn't hook me.

No one was home when I got there, so I put on my running shorts and shoes, covered my bare skin with sunscreen, pulled down the bill of my cap, and went for a run. A long run. A very long run. But the melancholy followed me like a dog on a leash—*if the cancer comes back*.

By the time I got home, it was nearly dark and my wife's car was parked behind my truck in the driveway. My knee ached again, as I climbed our front porch steps. My daughter let me in. She was thirteen. And wearing a bra now. They ought to make those damn things cancer-proof. That'd be a Wonder bra.

"Hi, Dad. How was your run?"

"I don't know."

She screwed up her face. "You're so weird."

"Where's your brother?"

"At the Mall with Valerie." My son was seventeen. Valerie was his girlfriend. She drove a hot yellow, convertible Mustang, which made my wife uneasy. "Mom's in the kitchen."

But I had already smelled our dinner on the stove, where my wife was grilling a salmon steak in a black, frying pan. I leaned against the door frame, watching her carefully flip the big, red piece of fish with the spatula. Truly, she was a beautiful woman.

"Smells good."

"Oh." She flinched, looked over at me. "I didn't hear you come in."

"Sorry. Didn't mean to startle you."

She turned to get something from the sink, stopped, stared back at me. "What?"

"What 'what?'"

"What are you looking at me that way for?" She eyed me suspiciously.

"Just looking." I grabbed a quart bottle of Gatorade—Cool Blue—from the refrigerator and unscrewed the top.

"Oh, Margo's housekeeper called. Something about an automatic cat box? She said you'd know what she meant."

"Yeah. I know." I took a big gulp of the cold, pale blue liquid, then remembered—*How soon? How soon?*—and I laughed again.

"What's so funny?"

"'Ees secret.'" I took another sip, then before leaving to shower, leaned against the door frame and asked my wife: "You busy Saturday night?"

She answered with a question: "Why?"

Plucking Sunflowers

by Cathleen Wedeking

I don't suppose the entry into the natural world is what anyone expects. It's scary at best, that is, until you feel the touch of a parent's soft fingertips caressing your face and that familiar voice calls your name for the first time.

They were both there when we arrived, our mother and father; both tired and sweaty, as if they had been working hours before we came along. Despite that, they met our requests for warmth.

Dad wiped our mother's forehead with a cool wet cloth.

"Is there anything you need?" he asked, his gaze slowly leaving her and resting on us.

She mumbled for ice water.

"Yes, of course," he whispered.

He wet the tip of his thumb with his tongue and cleaned away blood and mucus from my twin sister's left eye. He tightened my blanket and pulled snug my cap to keep my tiny head warm.

That was fifteen years ago. And now my twin, Abbie, and I sit on the porch swing enjoying the smell of fresh picked sunflowers from Grand Dad's country yard. She twirls a flower in my face and makes my nose dance from the digested fragrance, weakening my self-control.

"Abbie, stop," I demand. She giggles. She plucks one of the bright yellow petals and drops it to the weathered boards below.

"Alex, do you think--"

She plucks another petal, adding to the pile beneath her. "Do you think he loves her?"

Twirling a flower between my palms, I swing back and forth using my tiptoes to push off. I pull one of the petals off and throw it in her hair. "What in the world are you talking about?"

"I mean Dad. Do you think he loves Mom?" I try to swing faster, wobbling my sister's head, trying to make her grab for the armrest.

"Abbie, I don't know."

The next day, he holds the door open for her. He catches her elbow when she almost trips and falls, rushing to answer the phone. I study his face. Even after 20 years of marriage his eyes light up and the corners of his mouth curve, expressing delight in touching her.

From stories told, we know that the year they were courting, they spoke or saw each other every day. The careers they'd spent so much time growing and pruning took a back seat to long romantic dinners, leisurely hand-in-hand walks, and watching old movies while spooning on the couch. When the ring slid to the base of her delicate finger, ease and acceptance of their future together overtook them.

I blink my eyes to jar my thoughts. A memory of a fuzzy yellow petal, drifting too close to my eye, demands my attention.

Mom grips the phone in both hands and struggles to breathe as she consumes the words coming over the line. Now he wants to shake her.

"What is it!" he yells. He cracks his knuckles and paces in an erratic pattern. The tension builds in his body until he finally yanks the phone from her.

I try to justify his actions. These are conditioned responses, I tell myself. Dad is the protective, older brother of a mentally-challenged sibling. But his impatient expression washes away any level of concern.

Driving to the hospital, he holds her hand. His wedding ring almost disappears into hers and he speaks softly to her.

We have seen them play out this same scene before, but never as intensely as in the photos portraying my parents infertility struggles. At the insistence of our artistic Aunt Ashley, my mother agreed to let her tell the story of their desperate journey to conceive at the advanced age of forty-five through photos and documentation, later presented in a baby scrapbook. She assured her it would be a valuable memento, no matter the outcome.

The old photos revealed more hair and less wrinkles. In them he snuggled her, kissed her neck, and intertwined their hands until her tears stopped and their grief melted, birthing energy to continue the fight. Like many books, this one ended happily with new life-- times two.

They both watch my mother's brother's chest to ensure it continues to rise and fall. My mother cries continuously. It grates on my dad's nerves. He grinds his teeth and rolls his eyes. He pushes her hand away from his. Observing his diminishing strength is like being forced to watch an immovable hour glass, each piece of trickling sand predicting the withdrawal of his support. He walks to the vending machine, refuels on pretzels and apple juice and talks football with another husband, leaving my mother to contemplate the possibility of withstanding the loss on her own.

Dad loiters in the hallway, waiting for his supportive sister. She cups the back of his head in her right palm, and whispers, "You have to be strong for her now."

His glossed-over eyes clear. Her words penetrate his ears, and cake themselves onto his eardrums. He understands. Of all the admirable qualities my father possesses, being a quick learner serves him the best.

Many laughed at the notion of my father pursuing my mother with the intent to marry, saying, "She's too good for you!" or "Who do you think you are?" Despite the mocking, he leapt forward, learning everything about her and using it to his advantage. After learning of her gluten allergy, he signed up for a gluten-free cooking class to impress her with a lavish birthday dinner.

Chest puffed with confidence, he would joke, "Who says an old dog can't learn new tricks?"

He gathers his thoughts before entering the room again. He braces my mother's shoulders, leans toward her ear and speaks gently.

"Is there anything you need?"

He loves her.

As I Sit Here At The Computer

by Shauna McCahill

I am sitting here at the computer, aimlessly trying to think of something worthwhile to write about. All that comes to mind is that day at the hospital when they told me, "Don't worry, she isn't going to die."

Don't worry, they said. *She isn't going to die.* My knees buckled under the weight of those words. They couldn't be saying those words, not to me. My darling baby, the baby whom I'd dreamt of for years, whom Id fought to bring to life...wasn't going to die?

Of course she wasn't going to die. She was here because I willed her here. I willed her to be here. I wouldn't allow her to leave. From the start, it had been a battle to bring her into existence.

First there was the bleeding. They said it was just some spotting - to be expected at such an early stage. And with me having had so many pregnancies, and at my age (as if 34 was old by any stretch), well- it wasn't uncommon for breakthrough bleeding to occur when the fertilized egg implanted.

Next came the headaches. The awful, crippling headaches. They rendered me helpless when they hit. The doctor couldn't find an answer, could not find an explanation. He ran a CT scan and it showed nothing. They told me to drink more water. They told me to get more rest.

A month or two went by, and an ultrasound told me she was small. Not gaining weight properly. What was I doing wrong? They told me I was doing nothing wrong. Sometimes these things happen. *Sometimes these things*

happen? "She might even come early," they said. "But we need to know when she'll come so we can plan." They sent me home to rest. And to wait.

We needed to know when she was coming so they could give me the antibiotics. I had tested positive for Group B Strep and this meant having antibiotics before the baby came out so she wouldn't be born with meningitis. The doctors told me many women have it. As long as we got a couple rounds of antibiotics in before the baby came, she should be all right. The GBS shouldn't adversely affect her, nor should the antibiotics. The drugs needed to be administered while in labor but before it was time to push. This is what they told me.

I woke early one morning a few days before her due date. I felt the contractions growing stronger quickly. I went to the hospital and they put me on an IV. Within three hours I felt like it was time to push. But we had only managed one round of antibiotics so far. She was coming too fast, too fast to get all the antibiotics in.

She came quickly, but not easily.

For a moment, her head got stuck. And during that moment, air wasn't getting to her lungs. They said no damage was done. But when she was finally all the way out, she wasn't breathing. They turned her little blue body upside down. They shoved a suction cup down her throat and up her little nostrils.

Finally! That most glorious sound, her first cry! She didn't sound like all my other babies though.

They said it was fine. She was a different baby. "All babies sound different," they said.

To me, she sounded off in some way. None of my other babies had a voice quite so shrill, so distant. But she was here, and she was alive. She had made it. And for that, I was grateful.

Those first six weeks were very hard. She didn't sleep but an hour at a time, if that. I nursed her as best I could, but eventually I had to go to formula. I got no rest. I had others to think about too.

Thanksgiving came.

She was resting on her uncle's chest in a soft down blanket he'd bought for her. She'd been asleep for a few hours like that. At first, no one noticed. We'd assumed she was tired from all those sleepless nights. I was tired too. But the minutes and hours ticked by. I went over and took her off of him. She felt warm. I carried her little body upstairs and laid her on the bed. I wanted to get her moving, to look into her eyes, to wake her and feed her. But she just laid there like a tiny rag doll. She was hot when I took her clothes off to change her. She opened her eyes and they were glazed over. She didn't look at me, but past me and up to the ceiling. Her eyes rolled into the back of her head.

I grabbed the phone. *Why was she so listless?* I called my husband home from work. We took her to the ER.

The next few hours-- the next few days-- all became a blur. As I try to recall them now, they still seem fuzzy. We were at one hospital for a couple days. They told us she had an infection. A kidney infection, an E. Coli infection in her kidneys. That's what they said it was.

They asked me if I'd tested positive for GBS when I was pregnant. I said yes but that I'd been given antibiotics. *Only one dose though. She'd come too quick for the second dose.*

They put all these wires and needles into her little arms. They poked a needle into her spine. They said she didn't have meningitis. They took x-rays and said her lungs were filling with fluid. She had a fever. She had an infection. Damage was being done. *Irreversible damage?* My heart was stressed.

They put her in a helicopter and I flew with her to a second hospital. A special hospital for very sick children. They raced her down the hall to the NICU. I did not, would not, leave her side.

A doctor came in after the nurses. So many nurses! All those needles and wires. She looked so tiny in that crib. That cold, sterile crib.

She was only six weeks old.

One of the doctors stepped towards me after reviewing the ever-present chart at the end of her hospital crib.

He said, "Don't worry. She isn't going to die." *What? Can you repeat that please?* "Her heart has sustained some damage due to the infection in the kidneys. We'll give her medication to clear up the infection." *How did she get the infection?* "E. Coli is not a hard infection to get. It can come from an improperly changed diaper; it can come from many things. But in a baby this small, it is quite serious. Her lungs have filled with fluid. The medicine will help clear them up. She may have problems having babies later on in life." No one ever explained to me why. "She will need to go to a heart doctor before she ever goes to the dentist because she has a hole in her heart. It should close up on its own, eventually."

Should close up on its own? What causes it? Stress? Having given birth multiple times? Advanced maternal age?

We stayed in this hospital for two weeks, my baby and I. Knowing she would live, but not knowing what her quality of life would be.

I wondered if it was my fault. The early onset bleeding, the headaches, the low weight, the quick delivery. *Only having time for one round of antibiotics.*

I stayed up at night and watched her as she laid there, a helpless angel.

Finally they told us we could go home and resume our life. But the doctor's visits would continue, and frequently, through the rest of her childhood. Checkups for her heart, checkups for her kidneys, checkups to make sure she progressed developmentally. All this because of that one illness. All this because of things that should've been all right.

Now, years later, my dear daughter is still with us. She has a seizure disorder. She's been diagnosed with autism. She has a herniated bellybutton. They say that's due to the stress she endured, being so very sick as an infant.

She's not like other children. She doesn't sound like them. She doesn't behave like them.

They say her heart is fine, but I'm not so sure. The day we last had her checked, she wouldn't stop screaming. How could they have definitively heard if her heart was beating properly or not?

Don't worry. She isn't going to die.

That's what they told me. What they didn't tell me was what the outcome would be.

Sometimes I guess these things just happen. This is what I tell myself as I sit here at the computer, aimlessly trying to think of something worthwhile to write about.

◆———————————————◆

A Christmas Memory

by Michael Campagnoli

It's a day more than fifty years ago. I'm standing in the hallway of an old house. A modest house but richly appointed. Eastlake moldings, hardwood floors, pocket doors, stained glass. It reminds me of the Catholic church where he took me once, dark, foreboding, full of shadows and muted light. Old-fashioned, even then. Not unlike the man who lives there. The man is my grandfather. I'm standing in the hallway, peeking around the corner at him. He's naked to the waist, a towel stuffed in his trousers, and a straight razor in one hand. He peers into the steamy bathroom mirror. There's a cup on the shelf before him along with a bar of shaving soap and a brush. Nearby, a leather strop is bolted with a silver loop to the faded pearl-colored wainscoting. In an adjacent room, a suit coat, tie, and white shirt are laid out neatly on a bed. Somewhere in the house music plays.

The music is strange. A language I don't understand. Later I will learn it's the "E lucevan" from Tosca. I associate this music almost exclusively with him.

He pulls at his face, examines it in the mirror. A good face, symmetrical, wide lips and dark alert eyes. The lips are slightly parted. The nose prominent. A powerful statement. The mouth is never very far from a smile. He picks up the brush, urges the soap into the tough grain of his chin. When the face is properly lathered, he leans over the sink, raises the edge of the razor to the end of one sideburn, and the ritual begins.

He's not a big man. But even in advanced age, he's strong. A body capable of tremendous leverage. The hands are large and muscular, deeply creased. A stonecutter's hands. Dangerous. Even in repose, they carry the threat of violence. Once, I saw him knock a stranger out with a single blow. The stranger was taller, but the punch broke his nose like a rock crushing a biscuit. There was the crack of bone on bone, the snap-crackle of collapsing cartilage. The stranger's eyes rolled up in his head. He fell to the ground with a thud. There was shouting. People running. Blood everywhere. But now, as the music plays, the unquiet hands remain at ease.

Soft light pours into the coffin-shaped room from a sheer-curtained window. The music lifts and flows. The old man inclines his head to one side. Occasionally, he hums. At one point, his eyes turn pensive and slowly blink. They seek.

The tenor recapitulates and concludes.

Tosca is followed by a polonaise.

Grandfather, Nonno I call him, pursues the flat planes and fallen angles of his face. The razor rises and falls. He grimaces and scowls. There are long-slow and quick efficient strokes. The jaw is pushed and prodded. Folds of skin—pale at the neck—are menaced by the blade's bare glint. Pleasure is taken from the scrape and glide. The smooth white soap is pleasing against the darkness of his skin (especially where the skin is drawn tight at the brow and orbitals, the pronounced, accipitral cheeks). When the ritual's complete, the old man wipes the soap with a towel. Rinses with warm, then cold water. He slaps his face with lineament, powders his neck with talc, runs a comb through grey and thinning hair. Outside, there's silence. December shadows growing long.

Amid the rise and fall of Verdi and Caruso, he soaks peaches in his wine, dreams of the Old World, and a wife already dead from consumption. A thick, calloused finger traces the outline of a black, gilt-framed photograph. He talks of summer evenings. Just a young man, still a boy. Courting my grandmother, Raffaela.

Standing in moonlight beneath a Florentine window, he plays a barrowed mandolin, sings the passionate, "Maria, Mari!" or the simple, "Una furtive lagrima." Serenading. As his father before him, and his father, and his father's father. The scratchy music plays. Nonno leans his head back. His white mustache shines in the receding light. His dark eyes close. He looks old, fine-boned, and frail.

Standing in his bedroom, he folds the stiff collar of his shirt. He cinches a red, blue, and gold-trimmed tie into a slender knot. He straightens the knot and tightens it. Two black garters are slipped over the sleeves of his shirt and suspenders cinched at his waist. He lifts a deep blue suit coat from the back of a nearby chair and pulls it on. He straightens the coat and tugs gently on the starched cuffs of the white shirt.

In the living room, he stands before a chest-high, wood paneled Philco. Before turning one of the large dark brown knobs, he pauses for a passage by Respighi. Beniamino Gigli sails higher and higher. "Dell'aere ai morsi crudi," he cries and the old man, in the empty house, answers—

Gli addolorati tronche
offron pregando i bronchi
nudi.

How cold I am! How alone;
through the grey sky

a sigh flies up
from the dead.

It calls to me: Come,
the valley is dark.

Oh sad, unloved one,
come! Come!

The last remaining rays of the sun fill the room. His crooked figure sways gently in the dying light, dancing alone. Those hardened, ominous hands gesture plaintively, delicately, with a wild, knotted, sinewy grace. The final crescendo bursts, severs the air, is followed by a solemn coda. "Basta," the old man whispers, "Basta." Then he sees me in the half-shadows of the hall. Head bowed, eyes closed, I can feel his gaze upon me; the intensity of his heart.

A moment passes.

I look up, tentative, almost mournful, silent. Those dangerous hands hover not far from my head. The moment extends. Then, when neither he nor I can stand a moment more, he swoops down, grabs me in a rush, sends me squealing into the air.

"Buono Natale!" he says

Notes Editors & Regular Contributors/Columnists

Harmoni McGlothlin, Editor-In-Chief

Harmoni McG founded The Grace Notes Foundation in 2007 to benefit creative writers and to support the art of storytelling. As an award-winning screenwriter, fiction author, and poet, she often prefers delusions to reality. However, she often chooses red wine over both delusions and reality. Her books *Venus Laughs* (collected poetry) and *Soap In My Eye* (children's picture book) are both available now at GraceNotesBooks.com.

In 2011 Harmoni's screenplay Dumping Dick finished in the top 2% for the Nicholl Fellowship; a competition for unproduced scripts hosted by The Academy of Motion Pictures—that's "The-Guys-Who-Give-Out Oscars" to most folks. Another of her scripts is currently in negotiations for sale and an upcoming production.

Steve Karpicz, Prose Editor

Steve shot to success at an early age. His first novel, "The Moose, the Cow, the Accordion Player, and the Pickle" was a best seller in his second grade class. After retiring for several years, he once again picked up the pen. This time he made a name for himself in non-fiction, where through his work he helped several of his peers obtain their high school diplomas. Eventually the market bottomed out though, forcing Steve to pursue several other careers – customer service, bus driving, and movie theater projectionist to name a few - before he ultimately realized that he could think of nothing finer to do all day than to sit and stare at a blank page and draw funny doodles in the margins of crossword puzzles. His new novel, "Giving Good Head: The Mad Scientist's Guide to Constructing Your Perfect Date" is due out sometime in early 20xx.

Steven M. Grant, Poetry Editor

Steve is an award-winning poet living in New York City. His poems have appeared in The Writer, Spring Harvest, The Ampersand (&) Review, VVC Drama & English Literary Journal, Vivid Online Journal, and Drink This Cola. He graduated from a school you've never heard of with so many majors that even he is confused about his degree. His book, *Another Hotel Room*, is available through GraceNotesBooks.com. Before Joining Notes Magazine, Steve won The Golden Grace Note in poetry at our online writing community, NotesAndGraceNotes.com.

Shawn Maddox, Poetry Editor

Shawn is a multiple award-winner in the poetry category at notesandgracenotes.com, our online writing workshop. We found her work so compelling and her feedback to other poets so insightful, that we asked her to join our staff. She is the newest edition to Notes Magazine and we welcome her warmly- and patiently await the bio she seems to be having trouble writing.

Murvel Thornton, Poetry Editor

Murvel Thornton was our Featured Author for issue #2 and volunteered as a guest editor for the following issue. Eventually we begged him to stay on permanently and he agreed.

He is currently studying Sustainable Life Design and Application at Southwestern Oklahoma State University in Weatherford, Oklahoma. He plays often with mud and sand, and has been known to build habitable structures from paper and straw, using only a hammer and saw. A Montana native, Thornton has traveled the Pacific Northwest and California extensively, and knows the location of a number of secluded hot-springs in New Mexico. Being partial to organic farming, Thornton specializes in growing award winning sweet-potatoes, and cayenne peppers. Having exceeded the half-century mark earlier this year, he found an old stash and is quietly training to finish a marathon in the spring.

Adam T. Sullivan: Goodbye, Cruel Words

Adam T. Sullivan is not a character artist in Winter Park, Florida. He is neither a news anchor in Burlington, Vermont, nor an acoustic guitar player in New York City. He is the other one. There has been some confusion. This has led to the creation of adamtsullivan.com. We hope this clears things up.

Issue 5 Prose & Poetry Contributors

Spotlight Author: Suvi Mahonen holds a Master's degree in Writing and Literature from Deakin University in Australia. Her writing has appeared in a number of literary magazines and online in Australia (Island, LiNQ, Verandah), the UK (East of the Web), the United States (most recently on MetroMoms), Canada (All Rights Reserved) and Chile (Southern Pacific Review). She has also worked as a journalist in Australia and Canada and has published many feature articles, reviews and travel stories. One of her short stories, 'Bobby', was included inThe Best Australian Stories 2010.

Plucked Sunflowers: Cathleen Wedeking is a freelance writer and poet from the adventurous state of Colorado. She enjoys writing, not only for therapeutic reasons, but as a creative outlet and a desire to entertain and educate others. Her writings include flash fiction, short stories, ghostwritten articles, poems, greeting card verses, and her blog @
www.blogmusingsofanothermidlifer.blogspot.com
In her spare time, she takes pleasure in cooking, baking, hiking, bicycling, and caring for her loving husband and beautiful blue doberman.

Another Year Wiser: Kim Rock is a current full-time student at the University at Albany and a part-time peddler of moderately priced caffeinated beverages. Her writing is inspired by real life events, so she hopes to always be experiencing something interesting. Further samples of her work can be viewed at the blog she maintains, clevermouthwords.tumblr.com.
She can also be contacted directly, at kr425776@gmail.com.

Christmas Memory: Michael Campagnoli has worked as a waiter, fisherman, journalist, painter, and short-order cook. He taught literature and writing at Indiana University while studying for a Ph.D. His works have appeared in *New Letters, Southern Humanities Review, Red Rock Review, Natural Bridge, Crab Creek Review, Ellipsis, Emerson Review, Saint Ann's Review, Rattle, Blue Earth Review, Vermont Review, Yellow Medicine Review, Chaffey Review, New Madrid Journal, Tule,* and elsewhere. He has published three chapbooks *Ahmeddy-ga* (2005), *Loons* (Pudding House Publications 2008), & *Penobscot Voices: Kikukus* (Amsterdam Press 2009). Finishing Line Press will be publishing a new chapbook, *Silence & Dreams*, in 2013. His stories have appeared in the anthology, *Best New Writing of 2010* and ISFN's, *Anthology #1*. Three of his poems have been nominated for a Pushcart Prize.

Measuring Light: A former teacher, Elizabeth Varadan's stories and flash fiction have appeared in *The Rockford Review, Word Riot, Art Times, Long Story Short, Flash Me Magazine, Epiphany, Melic Review, Whim's Place, Laughter Loaf, Banyon Review* and *C-Oasis*. A short story, "Dragons", won honorable mention at the Jack London 9th Annual Writers Conference, 1997 and "Measuring Light", won special honorable mention in the February, 2006, Byline short story contest. Follow her on the web at:
twitter.com/4thWishVaradan
www.facebook.com/ElizabethVaradanAuthor
elizabethvaradansfourthwish.blogspot.com

The Facts Of The Case: Neil Mathison is an essayist and short-story writer who has been a naval officer, a nuclear engineer, an expatriate businessman living in Hong Kong, a corporate vice-president, and a stay-at-home-dad. His essays and short stories have appeared in *The Ontario Review, Georgia Review, Southern Humanities Review, North American Review, North Dakota Quarterly, Agni, Under the Sun, -divide-, Bellowing Ark, Pangolin Papers, Blue Mesa Review, Blue Lyra Review,* and elsewhere. Forthcoming are essays or stories in *Northwind,* and *Blue Lyra Review*. His essay, "Volcano: an A to Z" was recognized as a "notable essay" in Best American Essays 2010. Neil lives and writes in Seattle and you can find out more at www.neilmathison.net.

As I Sit Here At The Computer: Because of her rather eclectic upbringing, Shauna McCahill's interests, passions, and talents are many. A published poet, author of short stories, articles, essays, and memoirs, her work can be found in many places. Most recently, she ghostwrote a biography for the actor Steel Chambers, and edited a book of memoirs for the actress Krista Woods (ake Augusta Rain) Along with being a writer, Shauna is a Reiki Master Teacher (energy healing work) and facilitates both Reiki healing sessions and the passing on of attunements in the Usui tradition. Shauna strives to bring a certain spiritual wisdom and awareness to all of her endeavors. Making her home in the northern Midwest with her husband Tim, their eight children, and several pets, Shauna enjoys traveling, photography, Yoga, reading, and dabbling in the arts. Find out more at www.facebook.com/shaunamccahill

2008 World Naked Bike Ride, Portland, Oregon: Carl Duzett is from Portland, Oregon. At a young age he was bitten by a radioactive writer and he's been scribbling weird crap ever since. He currently resides in Maryland with his wife and son. You can follow him online at cduzett.blogspot.com and @cduzett on twitter.

White Fields and Emerson: Saul Lemerond is currently working on a masters degree in creative writing at Central Michigan University. He has been published in the *Sheepshead Journal of the Arts, Drabblecast, Dunsteef, Temenos, Waterhouse Review*, and elsewhere.

Fever: A wife and mother confused and limited by the words themselves, Kate writes at WifeMotherExpletiving in order to keep her fingers in the sanity pot.
www.wifemotherexpletiving.blogspot.com

Pricks: Rick Monaco grew up in Northern California and now lives in New York City. His writing has appeared in the San Francisco Chronicle, 3am Magazine, and various literary journals. He enjoys running, grilled meats and dogs with large cinder block heads.

Still Life With Limbs: Anthony Murphy lives, writes and sometimes reads out loud in New York City.

More words can be found here at: johnnycashbackatm.blogspot.com

Escapes: USAF veteran Tony Brown, an East Carolina University journalism program graduate, has won contests by Art Forum and Union Writers and received honorable mentions in Writer's Journal and Writer's Digest. His work has appeared in Bartleby Snopes, In Between Altered States, Long & Short Review, Word Gumbo, Short Story Alley, Fifty Word Stories, Sleeping Cat Books, and Leodegraunce, FoliateOak, Vapid Kitten, The Write Place At the Write Time, Short-Story Me, Gemini, The Storyteller, Blink Ink, Whortleberry Press, and elsewhere.

Find Out MORE About Notes & Our Contributing Writers & Editors (in This Or Any Other Issue) @ www.GraceNotesBooks.com

www.ingramcontent.com/pod-product-compliance
Lightning Source LLC
Chambersburg PA
CBHW080544180626
46818CB00008B/3122